T0367520

A HAPPY DAY AT
LONGTOWN

A HAPPY DAY AT
LONGTOWN

WITH POEMS, SONGS
AND DECLARATIONS
BY TOM THOMASSON

TOM THOMASSON

A HAPPY DAY AT LONGTOWN
WITH POEMS, SONGS AND DECLARATIONS BY TOM THOMASSON

iUniverse books may be ordered through booksellers or by contacting:

iUniverse
1663 Liberty Drive
Bloomington, IN 47403
www.iuniverse.com
1-800-Authors (1-800-288-4677)

Because of the dynamic nature of the Internet, any web addresses or links contained in this book may have changed since publication and may no longer be valid. The views expressed in this work are solely those of the author and do not necessarily reflect the views of the publisher, and the publisher hereby disclaims any responsibility for them.

Any people depicted in stock imagery provided by Thinkstock are models, and such images are being used for illustrative purposes only. Certain stock imagery © Thinkstock.

ISBN: 978-1-4917-7381-9 (sc)
ISBN: 978-1-4917-7382-6 (e)

Print information available on the last page.

iUniverse rev. date: 10/07/2015

Table of Contents

Photo Credits

Most of the photos and images included in this book are from Thomasson/Lunsford family photo archives. In other cases, photos were donated for use in this project. Those photo credits and acknowledgements are shown below. All photos are being used by permission.

Images 1-1, 5-25 and 7-3 courtesy of *Cherokee Scout*

Images 2-2 and 2-3 courtesy of Joseph G. Sebren. Source material provided by Eddie Lunsford

Images 5-2, 5-3, 5-4, 5-5, 5-6 and 6-6 courtesy of Bonnie Palmer

Images 5-10 and 5-23 courtesy of Emma Hogan

Images 5-9, 5-11 and 5-24 courtesy of Kathy Collins West

Image 5-17 courtesy of J. B. Barton

Image 6-4 courtesy of Wanda Stalcup and Cherokee County Historical Museum

Image 6-5 courtesy of Davis Family. Source material provided by Michael Gora

Image 6-7 courtesy of Sony Music Corporation and courtesy of Revenant Records. Source material provided by Frank Mare & Malcolm Vidrine

Image 6-8 courtesy of Sony Music Corporation. Source material provided by a collector who asked to remain anonymous

Chapter 1

Introduction

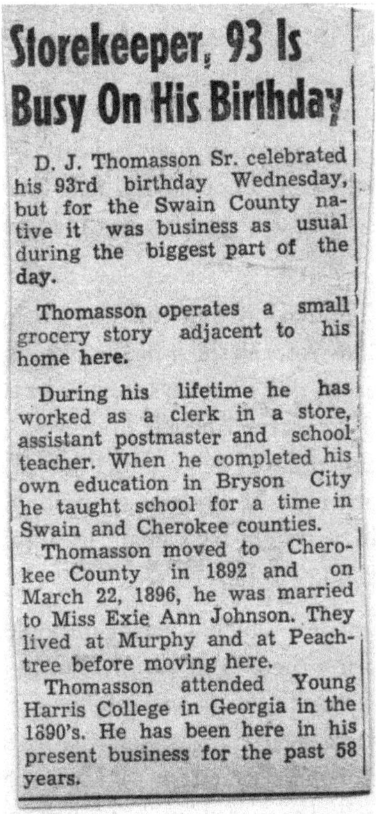

Storekeeper, 93 Is Busy On His Birthday

D. J. Thomasson Sr. celebrated his 93rd birthday Wednesday, but for the Swain County native it was business as usual during the biggest part of the day.

Thomasson operates a small grocery story adjacent to his home here.

During his lifetime he has worked as a clerk in a store, assistant postmaster and school teacher. When he completed his own education in Bryson City he taught school for a time in Swain and Cherokee counties.

Thomasson moved to Cherokee County in 1892 and on March 22, 1896, he was married to Miss Exie Ann Johnson. They lived at Murphy and at Peachtree before moving here.

Thomasson attended Young Harris College in Georgia in the 1890's. He has been here in his present business for the past 58 years.

Image 1-1: Aside from the minor indignity of having the first initial of his name typeset incorrectly, T. J. Thomasson was likely very proud of the above article printed in the local newspaper about 1963.

1

COMMENTARY: Chapter Introduction

Thomas Jackson Thomasson, Sr. was a man who lived in western North Carolina between the years 1870 and 1968. He was a gentleman farmer, a school teacher and a merchant. Those who knew him usually referred to him as "Tom" or more formally as "T. J." A number of people followed an old custom and referred to Thomasson as "Old Man Tom" or "Old Man Tom Thomasson." This practice has its origins in more formal sounding tags like "John the elder" or "Robert the younger." The point is that calling one "Old Man so and so" was not done out of disrespect. It was intended to be a gesture of honor or, at the very least, it served to separate one from their sons or other male relatives of the same last name. So, "Old Man Tom" was a friendly, respectful and practical title.

Tom Thomasson was born in Swain County North Carolina and later moved with his family to Cherokee County where he mostly remained for the duration of his life. Tom lived in a small community in Cherokee County informally known as "Longtown." He taught school in both Swain and Cherokee counties for approximately 14 years. He had country stores in both counties as well. Tom Thomasson likely had at least one store in Graham County. He was also a member of the local Masonic Lodge for nearly 70 years.

Another of Tom Thomasson's pursuits was writing. He was a fruitful poet and songwriter. "He wrote all the time," one of his granddaughters said about him. Another noted that he always tried to be truthful and accurate in his writing when it concerned people and events. Tom Thomasson's media of choice appear to have been a pencil and a small, lined writing tablet. An enduring memory of Thomasson among his family has him sitting on his porch in a straight back chair, leaning backward, with the tools of the trade in hand.

Tom Thomasson made a habit of creating multiple, handwritten copies of his poems and sharing them with various family members. He often wrote letters to family and friends in verse. Short "post card poems" consisting of four or five terse stanzas were mailed to some far sites on the globe. A number of them were sent to a son serving in the military and to a daughter who had moved away. As with many good writers, Tom Thomasson tended to recycle what he thought were good key phrases or poetic lines. In one or two cases whole stanzas float among a few pieces of poetry like classic verses in honored folk songs.

With the expectation of writing for a larger audience, Tom often had typewritten copies of his poetry and his letters prepared. Most of this task fell to his granddaughter Sarah Jean (Tommie) Lunsford. A great granddaughter, Stella Ann Gregory, assisted with the typing too. Tom's granddaughter Leila, and his son Fulton, worked and typed diligently to document and preserve many of Tom's writings in the years immediately following his death. There is no doubt that other relatives helped to preserve and perpetuate Thomasson's work.

Tom Thomasson wrote about everything. He found poetry in his family, in the mountains where he lived, and in children. Like all skilled writers, his sources of inspiration and topics of reporting are sometimes surprising. In this collection of about 140 of his writings, readers will discover how electric fans, apple orchards and indoor plumbing caught his fancy. Some of Tom Thomasson's poems were deeply personal and not widely circulated. In one case, only a single copy was ever known to exist. A respectable number of his poems was published in local newspapers over the years. One of his songs, a hymn, gained regional acclaim.

The poems in this collection are organized by theme. In some cases the rubric under which a piece should be filed is not obvious. The seine of history effectively retains some things and fails to snare others. The various subjects of Tom's poems span nearly two centuries. It is believed that the pieces in this collection were mostly written between the 1910s and the late 1950s. Some may be older by decades. If a copy of the writing included a date, it is provided. Periodically, notes are included to help clarify content for readers. Also each chapter provides some commentary. It is hoped that such additions will provide context and detail to help broaden this collection's appeal.

A large amount of credit is due to a large number of people! Many, many people over many, many years have helped to preserve Tom Thomasson's written legacy. Others have recently assisted more directly in the preparation of this book. A "thank you" inventory always runs the risk of offending someone due to an unintentional omission. In random order:

Leila Young
Zora Thomasson Gregory
Towanna Best West Roberts
Tommie Lunsford Bumgarner

T. J. Thomasson, Jr.
Steve Morrow
Stella Gregory Capo
Naomi Lunsford
Ann Miller Woodford
Lucy Long Blanchard
Hildred Lunsford
Andrews Public Library Staff
Austin Brady
Mary Phillips Morrow
Nancy Proctor
Ruth Clark
Ora Thomasson Lunsford
Martha Gregory Postell
Margaret Ann Gee
Lillian (Lil) Long Love
Eddie Lunsford
Bonnie Palmer
Faye Lunsford Gregory
Fannie Moore West, her daughter and son-in-law
Emma Hogan
David Young
Cora Thomasson Lunsford Nichols
Barbara J. Wooten
Fulton Thomasson
M. J. Nickolls
Toby Silver
David S. Sebren
Jason Yonce
Joe Sebren
Jane D. Swan
Judy St.Clair Sebren
David Brown
Julie Yonce

Tommie

Tommie is my namesake. I think she is sixteen
I guess she is the smartest girl that I have ever seen
She does most of my errands and tries to do them well
Because I think she likes me. And that's the way she tells

She never fails to rally and does things in a whiz
She is as great in her sphere, as Truman is in his
She types off my poems, most everyone I've got
I guess she thinks she's paying me for wearing that gold watch

I told her she could wear it, when she was "sweet sixteen"
She has got the joke now on me, and tickled most P-green
When she gets the poems finished, we'll place them in a book
And have them quickly published, so everyone can look

We think the book will glitter, if we can fix it right
I guess, when it is finished, that it will sell a sight
Perhaps we'll divide the profits. If profits it will bring
Then I guess we'll be happy and all our poems sing

Introduction

Stella checks our poems
With care she looks them o'er
With careful observation
As she has done before

Perhaps you'll say they're silly
With some fictitious names
But if you'll study fully
You'll find some things explained

We know that we sometimes do
Exaggerate a bit
The things we have in view
Is make our rhythm fit

Now some are post card poems
And some are little rhymes
But each one carries with it
Some happy little chime

We hope you'll read them carefully
When you are all alone
Perhaps you'll get some ideas
That you can call your own

Please read this volume fully
And study well the lines
And when you feel despondent
Write us some little rhymes

Junior: October 18, 1945

I guess I'd better ring off now
I know I've wrote enough
Unless it was of some more use
You see it is all stuff

This is poem number ten
In all two hundred lines
I think that I had better stop
I know you think it's time

I've got the poem letters all
Somewhere in my room
I sent you to the cotton mills
While you were skipping school

I may gather them all up
And make a little book
So when we have no more to do
We can at them all look

I now park and close my gag
That may your time consume
Wade has landed on this side
And we hope to see you soon

Note: "Wade" refers to Wade Lunsford. He was the son of G. W. Lunsford who was married to one of Tom Thomasson's daughters. Like "Junior" Thomasson, Wade had been serving in the United States Navy.

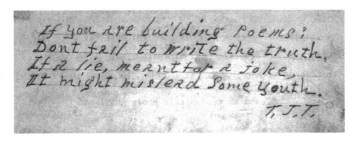

Image 1-2: Words of wisdom from Tom Thomasson.

Chapter 2

Tom's Heritage, Bryson City to Peachtree

COMMENTARY: Chapter Introduction

At about the time plans for the formation of a new western North Carolina county were unfolding, Thomas Jackson Thomasson was born. He entered life on December 11, 1870. Technically, Swain County did not exist until 1871 when portions of the existing Jackson and Macon Counties were joined into a newly formed province. Initially the county seat was called "Charleston." Within 20 years the name was changed to "Bryson City."

Tom's family had been in the area for some time. His parents were Lemuel Levi and Sarah Jane Davis Thomasson. Sarah Jane and her husband, sometimes called "Toby," were the parents of thirteen children. All of the children were born in or near the present day Swain County, NC area between 1860 and 1888. The children's names were James, William L., Solomon D., John A., Tom, Myra R., Charles W., Minter, Callie, Henry P., Benjamin A., Maggie and Mattie. Benjamin died in infancy. All the other children lived into adulthood.

For reasons undiscerned, Toby Thomasson moved his family to Cherokee County in North Carolina by around 1890. The family joined other early citizens of the neighborhood known as "Peachtree." It had a post office at one time but today is recognized as an unincorporated community. It does have a school, along with several businesses. Many of the children of Toby and Sarah Jane remained in the western North Carolina area. Some lived and worked for a time in mills at Gastonia, NC. Others settled westward in Texas and Oklahoma. The family maintained extensive land holdings in the Peachtree Community, some even into modern times. Visits to the homes of Swain County relatives, and other nearby haunts, were made throughout Tom Thomasson's life.

A particular piece of property at Peachtree was evidently a special family favorite. Its exact location has been lost to time. Perhaps no person now alive remembers it at all. Tom and his family called it "the camp," "the campus" or "the cabin." From Tom Thomasson's poetry (and from dim, second hand recollections) this property could best be described as a beautiful, rustic retreat. There was reminiscence of a mill pond and massive white pine trees. The original use of the property is unknown. It apparently remained in the family for years. Tom (with his wife and children and other relatives and friends) regularly visited for picnics, sleepovers and campouts. During the World War II era, in a series of "post card poems" Tom wrote to his son (T. J.) about his possible future use of the site.

In about 1896 Tom Thomasson married Exie Anna Johnson. She was a daughter of Francis and Sarah Jane Puett Johnson. Exie was orphaned by the time she was thirteen years of age. She and Tom Thomasson had seven children. One of the sons, Floid (sometimes spelled the traditional way, "Floyd") was stricken with meningitis in early infancy and died of resulting complications at the age of 16. Floid was never able to speak or walk. The other children were Zora, Fulton, John Henry, twins Cora and Ora; and T. J. Thomasson, Jr. All the children were born in the Peachtree Community. The family remained there until the mid to late 1920s.

While living at Peachtree with his own family, Tom Thomasson mostly made his living by teaching school. He also had country stores in the Peachtree Community and one at Marble, NC. It is of note that even today, Peachtree is divided into "lower" and "upper" districts for the sake of convenient geography. Tom taught school in the Slow Creek Community for years. "He'd walk across the mountain from our old home place [on Peachtree] every morning," recalled his daughter Ora.

This chapter offers works connected to Tom Thomasson's early childhood and youth at Swain County, and some related to his time at Peachtree. As noted previously, he often went back there for work and recreation.

Tommie's Great, Great Granddad – Esq. Jim

We claim much inheritance
From our Grandfather Jim
Who wrote and sang sweet poems
Much credit goes to him

He was Tommie's Great, Great, Granddad
And was of Irish descent
We hear his brogue in Tommie's voice
And know he was God sent

He was tall and very handsome
His hair was silver gray
He was a splendid, good old boy
Most everyone did say

Esq. Jim was recognized as the law
He always stood for right
He asked for nothing but the clean
And for the clean he'd fight

We dedicate these lines to him
He's long been gone away
But our Great, Great, Great Grandchildren
May read these rhymes someday

Note: "Tommie" was a nickname for Sarah Jean Lunsford, Tom Thomasson's granddaughter. James Madison (Jim) Thomasson (1809 – 1891) was recalled in this charming ode to Tom Thomasson's heritage. According to details of a widely circulated story, Jim Thomasson's wife Susannah Rebecca Truitt (1817 – 1890) marked the location she selected for her gravesite in Swain County with a firm impression of her shoe heel in the ground. She was dead within days. At her request the cemetery was originally called "Thomasson Cemetery." The name was later changed to "Sawmill Hill Cemetery."

A Little Boy's Prayer and Faith

It was many years ago, when I was just a lad
My brother had a fever. I knew that he was bad
He lingered and he lingered for many, many weeks
He didn't have the color of blood upon his cheeks
One day they said "He's dying." The doctor gave him up
His people all were crying, they couldn't give him up.
I ventured right in crying. The doctor shook his head
I heard someone whispering, "I think he'll soon be dead."
He looked like he was dying. I thought I'd try to pray
I slipped away despairing and hid myself away
I went away in secret, got down and tried to pray
I said, "Lord cure my brother." 'twas all I knew to say
I fell right down on my knees, "Oh Lord" -- I think -- I said
"If you don't help my brother, I know he'll soon be dead."
"Oh Lord Jesus, Jesus Lord, I'm trying now to pray
Oh, Lord, save my brother's life" 'twas all that I could say
I just kept right on saying "Lord, hear my humble prayer.
Please, don't let my brother die. It's more than I can bear."
Then something told me plainly "Your brother will not die."
I hurried back to see him. My eyes were nearly dry
He rolled his eyes up toward me, as I was passing through
My mother followed closely, "Son, what are we now to do?"
Poor William is now dying," tears streaming down her face
She wrung her hands and crying, "We can't stay on the place."
"Now William is not dying; I know he's better now.
There is no need of crying, he'll get better by and by."
"The doctors say he's dying. He can't live through the day.
You know that he is dying, why do you talk this way?"
I know it was a wonder. Just why I wouldn't tell
I was just a little boy, but knew that all was well
My brother still is living, far over in the West
It has been 'bout fifty years, as far as I can guess

A True Story and a True Dream

'twas on the Tuckaseegee a mile below the town
That now is Bryson City, Dock Massy had to drown
He was an awful drunkard. The stream was out of banks
He cussed, and swore he'd cross it. He horse began to prance

Into the stream he started. His horse began to swim
Dock Massy then went under. That was the last of him
'twas in the winter season. The tide was very high
A lot of folks were watching, when Massy had to die

They hunted and they hunted; for weeks a lot of folks
They hunted for Dock Massy, 'til they give up all hopes
A woman had a vision. It was old Rachel Grant
She dreamed right where to find him. They wouldn't take a chance

"He's three miles down the river." She said with honest heart
"I saw him in my vision, beneath some chunks of bark.
I dreamed this very plainly. I know that he is here
I saw him in my vision as plain as any star."

They gave her no attention. She was a wee bit slack
She still with tears contended, "I know right where he's at."
She says, "I'll go right with you and show you, for I can
We'll know the rock above him by a big bank of sand."

They then went right on with her, just as the dreamer said
They found the rock and bank of sand that to his body led
She showed them just exactly where to let their hook down
They brought up his body the first time they let down

Note: Tom Thomasson elected to use fictitious names and changed two small details in this otherwise true story. The actual incident took place in the early 1880s.

Jack Lambert

It was at Bryson City, 'bout fifty years ago
Jack Lambert was convicted, as many people know
They swore he killed Dick Wilson, he swore it wasn't so
With evidence convicting, Jack Lambert had to go

The judge read out his sentence, "Now Jack, you'll have to die
Upon the murder's scaffold, between the earth and sky."
It was a sad occasion, to see that awful gang
Gathering 'round the gallows, to see that poor man hang

John Woodard preached his funeral. He made a strong appeal
Jack Lambert sat and listened. It was an awful scene
He read a verse of scripture, then for Jack Lambert prayed
He asked the Lord to save him. An humble plea he made

Then Lambert stepped forward, the people to address
He said that it was whiskey that caused him this distress
He said that it was whiskey that brought him to disgrace
Advising every other, that stuff to never taste

He pointed to the gallows tears streaming down his face
"Boys do not fool with whiskey, your parents to disgrace.
I did not kill Dick Wilson, you all may know someday.
But I am fully ready, the debt of death to pay."

The sheriff was so shaky, he couldn't hardly stand
But Lambert did assist him. He said, "Sheriff, tie my hands."
It was many years later, a comrade by the way
A comrade of Jack Lambert fell very sick one day

He said, "I am now feeling, the debt I one time made,
for killing poor Dick Wilson, Jack Lambert for me paid.
I know Jack is in Heaven. He was so true and brave;
He died upon the scaffold, my life he meant to save."

"Now life, with me, is over, if God will let me go.
'twas me that killed Dick Wilson. Let everybody know.
I killed him with Jack's pistol. Jack said he wouldn't tell.
Jack died upon the scaffold. Now I must go to hell."

Note: The subject of this set of verses is one of the saddest tales in the history of western North Carolina, the execution of Andrew Jackson (Jack) Lambert in July of 1886. A few detailed documents relating to this story have been preserved by Lambert's family and by local historians. The execution is said to have been witnessed by hundreds of people. The poem appears to have been written in the early 1930s. Given Tom Thomasson's age at the time of the Dick Wilson murder in 1884, it is possible that this poem could be a first-hand account of some of the resulting events. Tom may have personally known these people and he may have witnessed the execution of Mr. Lambert.

The School

The school here will soon be out
We kids will all be glad
We have had the biggest school
I guess we ever had

We all like to go to school
But we are just worn out
The most of us will get a pass
And that will be all right

Now we'll have a lot of fun
No matter what it takes
We all must camp and picnic
In several of our states

We'll have a splendid rest
We'll climb the mountains high
If we don't have a jolly time
Tell us the reason why

In Memory of J. M. Thomasson

September 20, 1954

Dear Minter's gone, just up above
From earthly pain to Heaven's love
His soul has flown to Heaven's shore
To be with loved ones evermore

God through his gracious love
Has taken him from worlds of pain
To Heaven's bliss above
Our loss is Heaven's gain

He was so kind and so devoted
God took him from us away
To be with Heaven's happy throng
Through one eternal day

We are lonely, Oh! so lonely
Since he went from us away
But we know that we can only
Look to God for help each day

Our hearts are sad beyond compare
But we'll submit to God's great will
Heaven's courts rejoice up there
We know he doeth all things well

His active life on Earth is o'er
But his kind words and deeds live on
His soul has flown to Heaven's shore
To be with Angels evermore

Our circle here is broken
We feel so lonely here
But we'll trust the promise spoken
Oh! may it not be broken there

Note: Joseph Minter (J. M.) Thomasson was Tom Thomasson's brother.

To Mrs. Pink Thomasson and Family

He has gone our precious husband
Our father and our brother, too
But we know someday we'll meet him
In the land beyond the blue

His kindly voice we cannot hear
His smiles we do not see
But in our hearts we have no fear
Those lovely smiles will always be

He was so kind, and so devoted
God took him, from us away
From Earth to heaven, his soul promoted
Where there is one eternal day

We are lonely, Oh, so lonely
Since he went from us away
But we know that we can only
Look to God for help each day

Our hearts are sad we think beyond compare
But your hearts are sadder over there
But let's submit to God's great will
Because he doeth all things well

We know the circle here is broken
Our hearts are lonely, lonely here
But we trust the promise spoken
Oh, may it not be broken there

Oh, may we, Nannie, Craig and Glen
Meet him above this world of sin
With mother in his arms of love
Where all is joy and peace and love

Note: William Pinkney Thomasson died in July, 1931 and is buried at Swain County, NC. His wife, Elizabeth, was often called "Lizzie." Pink was the son of Jake Thomasson and a cousin to Tom Thomasson. Pink and Lizzie had children Nannie and Glen. Nannie's husband was named Craig.

Keep Your Receipts

Dear Brother:

Be sure your rent receipts you keep, so that no other one can cheat
For then no one can pick a flaw and we would not feel half so raw
If any one of them you've lost; I'll duplicate, without a cost
With absolutely correct dates. I've got the stubs that for you wait

To itemize, I never failed, that you could see just every sale
Each week you looked them o'er and o'er. With your consent we said – no more
My confidence you fully gained, by your quick thought the one to change
By drawing naught around the one "With thanks" to prove, the date you'd won

Ten or eleven still remains. I'll tell the world I've never changed
It matters not what others say. It looks to us the same old way
You know we itemized each week, so if these lines you wish to keep
With satisfaction every time, to keep our problems all in line

A date to pay and one approve, is just the same but may confuse
It really means just two in one. This error we should always shun
"there's no one half so blind as he who don't even want to see
and harder to convince him still, of anything against his will"

Keep your receipts they always talk. For one receipt I received naught
(The twelfth and first) to "solnfy"; 'twill all be settled in the sky
I hope your moving satisfies; with me no evil thought survives
I hope your confidence I share and now may we part on the square?

Note: Events described in this story (was it a joke; an argument?) and to which brother of Tom Thomasson's the letter poem was addressed, are not known in detail. In the fourth stanza a proverb or old maxim is paraphrased. The meaning of "solnfy" is not clear.

Lieutenant Sam B. Gibson

A true story of the conversion of Lieutenant Sam Gibson, a wealthy merchant of the Cold Springs section of Swain County, NC:

Mr. Gibson was very wicked and would curse the church and everyone who approached him about his soul's welfare.

He wife, Mrs. Sarah Gibson, was a church worker.

A revival was going on at the Cold Springs Church and their four boys were at the mercy seats for the prayers of the church.

Mrs. Gibson, together with a number of Christian workers, coveted to pray for Mr. Gibson's conversion.

They met in a barn near the Gibson home and prayed fervently for his conviction and conversion.

A reluctant committee was sent to the home; they found Mr. Gibson rolling in his bed and crying for mercy.

He repented and turned to Christ, together with the whole family, and remained faithful to the end.

I was working for Mr. Gibson at the time and I know this story to be true.

COMMENTARY: *In Memory of Mother,* Sarah Jane Davis Thomasson

One of the earliest surviving writings of Tom Thomasson is, ironically, his best preserved and most widely circulated. After Tom's mother, Sarah Jane Davis Thomasson, died in 1909 Tom wrote a hymn based on her dying words to her family. Tom's daughter Ora noted that "...words in that song is words that she spoke."

Ora's twin sister Cora added "That's what my daddy said. And mother was there too." She [Sarah Jane] was laying in the bed and hadn't even raised up and moved in weeks...she shouted and laid back down. Now that's what Mamma said and I believe everything she said."

Tom Thomasson called the hymn *In Memory of Mother.* How he got the idea to submit the song for publication is not known. Tom was active in church and in the local music scene. He may have crossed paths with George W. Sebren or some of his business associates at a singing convention or he could have corresponded with him by mail. Sebren was a good songwriter and a pioneering gospel quartet singer. *In Memory of Mother* was printed along with a number of other lesser known hymns, and some classics, in a publication called *Beulah Songs.* It was a hymnal produced by Sebren's Asheville, NC based company. Another branch of the company was housed at Texas. Nestled among some of the great hymns like *How Beautiful Heaven Must Be, Blessed Assurance, Sweet By and By, Glory to His Name,* and *I Am Bound for the Promised Land* was Tom Thomasson's tribute to his mother and her Christian faith.

Periodically, a friend or relative would relate to Tom that his hymn was being sung at some regional church. Congregations in Cullowhee and Bryson City are known, for example, to have included the hymn in their choir's repertoire. As a singing leader Tom would often gather family and/ or friends together to sing for pleasure or home entertainment. On one such occasion, during a family picnic, a surprise rainstorm caused the family to stow a stack of their song books in a mailbox-like shelter they found nearby. After the storm broke the family drove away, accidentally leaving the hymnals behind. They were never able to recover their treasured books.

In Memory of Mother

Published by Beulah Songs, #8

Sometimes when I'm burdened with troubles and cares
As over this wide world of sorrow I roam
My memory turns back to my dear mother's prayers
She whispered "Dear children, come home."

REFRAIN

Then let us go home to the beautiful land
Beyond the radiant sky
In mem'ry we see mother's beautiful hand
Calling us there on high

She said she'd be watching at heaven's bright gate
For dear loving friends who had promised to come
She shouted the praises of god as she sang
And whispered "Dear children, come home."

REFRAIN
Dear father and brothers and friends have gone on
To join her in praises 'neath heaven's fair dome
I know I shall see her when earth-life is o'er
She whispered "Dear children, come home."

REFRAIN
I'll always remember the last words she said
Before she departed with angels to roam
She bade us "live close to the Master while here"
Then whispered, "Dear children, come home."

REFRAIN

Image 2-1: Sarah Jane Davis Thomasson pictured with an unknown child. She was the inspiration for the hymn *In Memory of Mother.*

Image 2-2: Cover Image for *Beulah Songs*.

Image 2-3: The sheet music for *In Memory of Mother* from the hymnal.

Tom Thomasson

About My Favorite Song

Dear Sis:

I'm glad they sing my song out there, the one composed of Mother's prayer
It makes me think my work lives on among some happy, happy throng
I wish they'd sing it all around, in every village and in town
It matters not who sent it there. I wish they'd sing it everywhere

It was composed of mother's prayer, the last one that she uttered here
There's many mothers gone before, with loved ones left the wide world o'er
The words selected all were so, the family circle full well know
We promised her both one and all, to meet her there when we are called

"Prepare" she said, "when I am gone, to meet me there around the throne
where all is joy and peace and love in that eternal home above."
She whispered softly "All is well. Farewell dear children, fare you well.
I'm going home to Christ above, where there is joy and peace and love."

I think I'll know my mother there; in Beulah land, somehow, somewhere
She will be waiting there I know because she plainly told me so
When we get there after a while morning will dawn, Heaven will smile
With loved ones there we all will dwell; all will be well, all will be well

Mother and Home

Mother's gone somewhere above to that home of peace and love
"I am going home," She said. "When my body here is dead."
Hear me Jesus now I pray, take me home with you today
Take me Jesus, take me home, there no trouble will be known

CHORUS: Home sweet home, oh home sweet home. Won't that be a wonderful home!

I remember very well when she said, "My boy farewell;
Meet me darling in that home where we'll know as we are known."
I am going over there to that happy home somewhere
We will sing around the throne, while eternal ages roll

CHORUS: Home sweet home, oh home sweet home. Won't that be a wonderful home!

Come on friends and go along. Won't you join our happy throng?
We'll be singing "Home Sweet Home" while eternal ages roll
Jesus loves our troubled souls, he will lead us to the fold
When we here no more shall roam He will take us over home

CHORUS: Home sweet home, oh home sweet home. Won't that be a wonderful home!

Note: This hymn is connected to "In Memory of Mother" in theme but does not appear to be directly based on Sarah Jane Davis Thomasson, Tom Thomasson's mother.

Junior: October 15, 1945

Your dad and ma and ma-in-law
All feeling very brisk
Went out to Bryson yesterday
To see J. Harold Smith

He preached and pranced all o'er the stand
We thought that he was grand
But when he got through we saw
That he was just a man

The "Carolina Watchman"
Was just about his theme
He had one of the biggest crowds
That we have ever seen

Your dad and ma and maw-in-law,
J. H. and Bennie Mae,
Was anxious then to get back
But Zeek just begged to stay

We all got home safe and sound
We had a splendid time
I'm sending poems up-to-date
You see I've got behind

Note: J. Harold Smith was a well known Southern Baptist evangelist in the region. He founded the "Radio Bible Hour" and was a pioneering religious television broadcaster. "J. H" refers to John Henry Thomasson, Tom's son. His first wife was Bennie Mae Holloway. The identity of "Zeek" is not known. "Bryson" of course, refers to Bryson City.

Junior: October 16, 1945

We had a big time at Bryson
J. Harold kept us late
We came back with John Henry
And there we each one ate

Aunt Jo fixed a good supper
The best we ever "eat"
We each one ate a plenty
You never saw the beat

We then put in tobacco
About a thousand sticks
It had to be protected
But made us each one sick

He then delivered dad and mom,
Also your maw-in-law
We took your wife some cabbage
To fix her up some slaw

If you don't like my poem gag
You'd better tell me why
For I may write another
About some other guy

Junior: October 17, 1945

When we left Bryson City,
My former county seat,
We everyone was talking
About J. Harold's speech

We motored through the village
Of all my childhood dreams
Where many memories linger
About my childhood scenes

A school house now is standing
Right on the very lot
Where I was born and "snaked up"
It is a lovely spot

Me thinks I see my grandpa Jim,
My mother and my dad
They were all, I surely know,
The best friends that I had

Our former "drunk" is teaching there
Peculiar – but a fact
He is telling them just what to do
And how they all must act

Dear Junior: June 26, 1934

Last week I went to Peachtree, the twenty-second of June
I put on two hundred buds. I'm sure they were all Junes
Won't that be a June orchard when they all make big trees?
I think they will all do well. The ground is sown in peas

The old trees are all doty, across the Moth Spring Branch
We'll cut them down this winter and give these Junes a chance
There was only one tree left, that had no science to boil
I peeled that tree all around. I did it with a spoil

If you want a good orchard, put in a splendid graft
Then cultivate that orchard and prune it every chance
If you don't bear some good fruit it's surely not your fault
You have had a splendid chance. Don't take the road that's off

Note: In the second and third lines, "Junes" and "June" refer to June apples. This variety bears fruit early, usually in the month of June. Doty [pronounced DOH-tee] is an old, local term that refers to decayed trees or lumber.

Junior: October 8, 1945

Your idea of the cabin
Indeed was quiet correct
About the Pilgrim Fathers
And about your architect

Your architect while thinking
About a proper lot
Thought of the Pilgrim Fathers
And freedom's happy spot

The big white pine was chosen
About its pleasant shades
Beside the trickling waters
The rustic camp was made

No spot could be selected
More private or complete
Where sweet breezes, though the pines
Would sing you off to sleep

Although it's weather beaten
It stands there by the pines
When you get home we'll fix it
We have that on our minds

Note: This is one of several "post card poems" Tom Thomasson sent to his son T. J. who was serving in the United States Navy during World War II. He also worked away from home for a time in his early civilian life. The subject of this poem, and the next three, is the Thomasson family retreat at Peachtree called a "camp" or "cabin" as discussed in the introduction to this chapter.

Junior: October 10, 1945

Your architect is thinking
Of the camp across the creek
And that if you'll repair it
You may have it all for keeps

I think it's worth protecting
For its architectural skill
It has no joints of rafters
But ribs that fill the bill

You can make it more attractive
By chinking all the cracks
Then paint the chinking yellow
And paint the poles all black

It should be a reservation
Although an abrupt spot
It is fine for the occasion
The best that we have got

It lies across the ripples
Beyond the little mill
You may keep this as your deed
Because it is my will

Tom Thomasson

Junior: October 12, 1945

Beyond the Peachtree valley
Beyond the rocks and rills
You'll find a pine pole cabin
Below the little mill

The location is peculiar
Selected for relax
Without the sound of traffic
To study nature's facts

The jaybirds in the treetops
The trout dart through the stream
The squirrels how they chatter
The like was never seen

When we have relaxed thoroughly
Enjoying nature's scenes
The rippling of the waters
Reveals to us sweet dreams

It holds some pleasant memories
Some pleasures of the past
We very well remember
The time we were there last

Junior: October 12, 1945 (#2)

We are always cogitating
Along life's weary way
Most always about something
That doesn't ever pay

Of course that's like the cabin
Without one cent of pay
But heaps of sports and pleasures
That helps us on our way

When we talk about the cabin
To which we often rode
We think about the builder
Two-fifths around the globe

It's less than Yokohama
But doesn't stink so bad
No doubt it is the best resort
That we have ever had

The camp needs some repairing
The foot log's fallen down
When you get home we'll fix it
And other things around

Peachtree Blues

I am going to Longtown
Where sweet girls are all around
They all treat me mighty well
There is no one here can tell

Chorus: I am leaving Peachtree soon. I can't stand these awful blues.

First I courted Mary Jane
Then I thought I'd make a change
You will see I'm not to blame
Faye is pretty just the same

Chorus: I am leaving Peachtree soon. I can't stand these awful blues.

There are others don't you know
I will court next time I go
I can never, never stay
From those pretty girls away

Chorus: I am leaving Peachtree soon. I can't stand these awful blues.

Won't that be a happy day
When at Longtown I can stay?
We will laugh and we will shine
We'll be happy all the time

Chorus: I am leaving Peachtree soon. I can't stand these awful blues.

I will tell you, yes I will
All about the little mill
From the mill you'd better stay
It will never, never pay

Chorus: I am leaving Peachtree soon. I can't stand these awful blues.

Note: This song was chosen as a closure to this chapter and as a way to mark a transition in Tom Thomasson's life. Details of his life in "Longtown" near Andrews, NC will follow in a subsequent chapter.

Chapter 3

Tom's Family, Part One

COMMENTARY: Chapter Introduction

As noted previously Thomas Jackson (Tom) Thomasson was married to Exie Anna Johnson Thomasson. Tom was born December 11, 1870 and lived to almost one hundred years of age. He passed away on October 28, 1968 at Andrews NC in the Longtown community. Tom's daughter Cora recalled asking her father, bedridden and ill, if he wanted to go to the hospital. "No, I want to go to heaven." was his reply.

Exie Johnson Thomasson was born April 4, 1876 and died December 2, 1955. As Exie grew older she began to be plagued by a tangle of health issues. These medical problems required extended hospital stays. This chapter includes what may have been Tom's final poem to his wife, *Dear Exie*. Tom memorialized Exie's passing and the details of her funeral in a separate account. Copies of that poem were typed on decorative paper and distributed among family members.

The present chapter will focus on Tom and Exie as well as their children. The oldest child was Zora Jane, born in 1896. She married John Berton (Bert) Gregory and spent most of her life at Andrews. The couple had a daughter, Stella Mae, and a son called "J. B."

Thomas Fulton Thomasson was Tom and Exie's oldest son, born in 1898. He married Leila Mason and had two sons, Billy and Charles. Fulton mostly stayed in western North Carolina but moved around a lot pursuing his work as an educator.

John Henry Thomasson was born in 1901. He also worked as an educator. He and his first wife, Bennie Mae Holloway, had one daughter named Patricia. Bennie Mae succumbed to tuberculosis and Patricia died at the age of 32. She was comatose as a result of encephalitis for many months prior to her death. She briefly emerged from the coma before passing away. John Henry married a second time to Ida McCabe Byrd. Prior to that marriage she had sons George and Wilton.

William Floid Thomasson was the fourth child. Floid was born in 1902. Sadly, he was severely disabled by meningitis during infancy. He died as a teenager in 1918 from pneumonia and other complications related to his infirmity. His death certificate included a notation: "Invalid all life." He was buried at Peachtree Baptist Church Cemetery.

A pair of twin daughters was born to Tom and Exie in 1905. Ora Augusta married George W. Lunsford, a widower from Andrews. The couple had five children. Naomi died in infancy. Others were Sarah Jean (Tommie), James W. and twins Loster and Leila. George Lunsford had nine children from his previous marriage: Dillie, Annie, twins Ray and Fay, Mary, Wilma, Wade, Jack and Cecil. Most of George's older children referred to Tom and Exie Thomasson as "Grandpa and Grandma."

Ora's twin sister was Cora Caroline Thomasson. She was married to Charles J. (Charlie) Lunsford who was a distant cousin of George Lunsford. Cora and Charlie had four children: C. J., Thomas Matthew, William Theodore (called "Billy Ted") and Ann. Cora was widowed but remarried later in her life to Chauncey T. Nichols who was called "Chan." Ora lived all her married life in Andrews. Cora settled there permanently in later years but also lived at Peachtree. She and her husband moved to Gastonia for a time, like so many other local families of the era, to find work in factories.

The youngest child born to Tom and Exie arrived in 1916. Named for his father, he was often called "T. J." or in his early years, "Junior." He served in the United States Navy and eventually had a lengthy career with the Tennessee Valley Authority (TVA). Glenna (Polly) Franklin was his wife. They had a daughter, Polly Ann, who died as a newborn. Other children from the marriage were Betty, Glenda, Roger and Jack.

There is no doubt that Tom Thomasson was lovingly proud of all members of his large family. He nurtured, encouraged and helped them in their lives. He was always quick to note their successes to friends and neighbors.

Image 3-1: Gravestone of Floid Thomasson, son of T. J. and Exie Johnson Thomasson.

Dear Exie

Dear Exie,

We were so glad to have you home and hope, you too, enjoyed each day
Please hurry up and get real well so you can come back home to stay
Your visit home was just too short but was the best that we could do
So do the very best you can, you know I'm thinking now of you

I'm mighty glad you got back safe and hope you are feeling fine
So when you get half a chance please write me just a line
Enclosed you'll find an envelope, addressed and stamped as you can see
That will tell the Government to bring your letter to me

Fond wishes from your loving husband

T. J. Thomasson

Andrews NC

10-10-1955

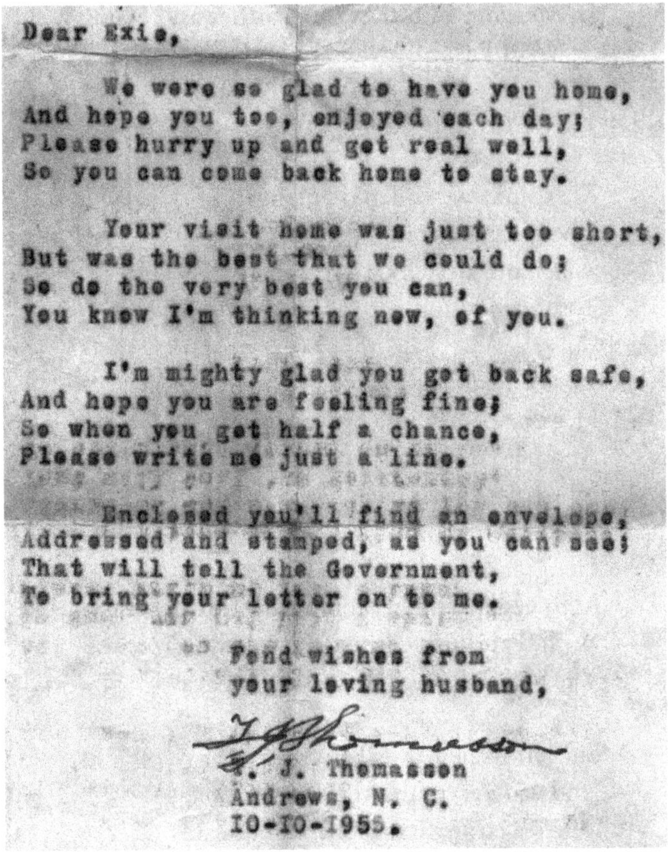

Dear Exie,

We were so glad to have you home,
And hope you too, enjoyed each day;
Please hurry up and get real well,
So you can come back home to stay.

Your visit home was just too short,
But was the best that we could do;
So do the very best you can,
You know I'm thinking now, of you.

I'm mighty glad you got back safe,
And hope you are feeling fine;
So when you get half a chance,
Please write me just a line.

Enclosed you'll find an envelope,
Addressed and stamped, as you can see;
That will tell the Government,
To bring your letter on to me.

Fond wishes from
your loving husband,

T. J. Thomasson
Andrews, N. C.
10-10-1955.

Image 3-2: Typed copy of the preceding poem, *Dear Exie.*

In Memory of our Wife, Mother and Sister
Who Passed Away December 2, 1955

April 4, 1956

Me thinks we will all remember
The second day of December
When our dear Exie left us here
To linger 'round her vacant chair

'twas on a lonely rainy day
Her grandsons bore her form away
And placed it in a silent grave
'til Christ comes back her form to raise

Her granddaughters, the flower girls,
Marched 'round her tomb with flowing tears
With tear dimmed eyes and solemn gaze
They placed sweet flowers on her grave

She left us here awhile to roam
And wander 'round the vacant home
Where sixty years we shared our cares
Together with our joys and tears

She has gone to see her mother,
Father, sister, son and brother
To be with them forevermore
On that bright celestial shore

Her soul has flown to Heaven's shore
To be with Angels evermore
Where all is joy and peace and love
In that sweet happy home above

Indeed, it seemed to us to soon
But God has made for her more room
He caused her toils and pains to cease
By giving her a home of peace

Oh! how we wished to keep her here
Because she was so very dear
But God saw fit to take her home
With angels evermore to roam

All our toils will soon be over
And we'll anchor up in glory
To be with God's bright Angel Band
Far above the Sinking Sand

Note: Some copies of this poem begin with the line "Of course we will all remember"

Wandering

Dear Twin:

Perhaps you've done the best you could.
But you could have stayed here if you would
So I would had on either side
a lovely "twin" my life to guide
But you so anxious to get rich,
just left a house that was well fixed
And went away back East to roam.
When you went broke I brought you home
I placed you back then on the farm,
a lovely spot where you were born
But when you saw no home for peace,
I blame you not for going east
The place has gone, just let it go.
We tried to prize things up we know
We did our best we're not to blame.
We did it all in Jesus' name

A few outlawed the place we know.
We thought it best to let them go
And let them do just as they would,
no matter where they each one stood
The farms have all about grown up,
the ones that once made such good stuff
We hate to see them go that way;
but nothing there again will pay
We'll hold the farms there in reserve,
for all their joys and all their tears
The little church that we all built,
is written there with perfect ink
Methinks I see the rocks and rills,
the camp below the little mill
The little church that we all built.
Methinks I see -- Methinks, I think

Dear Cora: October 2, 1936

This is Fulton's birthday. I think he's thirty-eight
We went to camp today and ate and "eat" and ate
We had squirrel and gravy, you never saw the beat
It was a splendid supper. We eat and ate and eat

We knocked about the campus, with Leila in the lead
Your mamma made the coffee, the best you ever "seed"
It was a fine occasion. Zora danced all around
Without exaggeration, she said she gained five pounds

You can bring your boys over as soon as you please
Your house will soon be vacant. You can rest at your ease
So no more at the present, guess you don't get my stuff
If not, it doesn't differ. You've not lost very much

Note: A reference to the "camp" and "campus" at Peachtree is explained in Chapter Two. Leila was Fulton Thomasson's wife.

Dear Cora: August 28, 1936

I understand you want to move, soon as Mr. Adams goes
Guess you need not wait for that so far as anyone knows
You can go into the camp. It is made of peeled pine poles
Between each pole there is a crack; there is no other holes

Your chatting now, I should think, will be all right to store
It might be best to change about and pay the rent no more
I suppose the old store house, the one I used to use
Would hold most of your junk 'til Mr. Adams moves

Get old "Trix" as you come by, for no one she will wait
To quickly look the campus o'er, to see there is no snakes
Let me know what you want, so I can "sorter" plan
If you want to come back home we'll do the best we can

Note: Mr. Adams was a neighbor at Longtown in Andrews, NC. "Trix" refers to Trixie, Exie Thomasson's dog. The meaning behind the phrase "your chatting" is not clear. An old legal term, chattel, may be what Tom had in mind while playing with the local dialect. That term refers to personal property such as furniture. Finally "the old store house" refers to a building in the Peachtree Community of Cherokee County where Tom Thomasson once had a country store.

A Mighty Big Lie

Junior said, sez he, "Hello there, Mr. Longfellow"

No I am not Longfellow, I hate it mighty bad
I heard him say the other day that you was his granddad
So he is my great-grandson. He went to my first school
He was a splendid good old boy and never broke a rule

I must have gained his confidence. He always praised my name
And he gave me full credit for all his noted fame
You are supposed to be my son. You know never to lie
But if a word of this is so, I wish that I may die

Image 3-3: Tom and Exie Thomasson are pictured with their son "Junior."

Dear Junior: May 12, 1934

We didn't get your letter 'til very late today
It went to South Carolina. From us it got away
But then it came back safely as you before replied
We was scared something was wrong or you would not have lied

Address your letters plainly when they contain such pay
Or they'll go to South Carolina. Don't let them get away
There's so many things happening, so many things that's true
We thought that perhaps something had there befallen you

I would have written sooner, but looking every day
For you to slip in on us. On that we went astray
Now we are doing nicely but lonely as can be
Your mama wants to see you. It's bad enough for me

Dear Junior: May 20, 1934

This is May the twentieth, nineteen and thirty-four
We sure did get your picture, you should have sent before
It looks exactly like you when you were just a boy
Your hat is most too broad though; your gun looks like a toy

We looked for you last weekend but though you didn't come
We heard that those on Peachtree was looking for their son
If you come in next weekend I guess we'll be at home
Just working in the garden; we hardly ever roam

You should be complimented for sticking to your job
Perhaps you'll be promoted. If not, it makes no odds
Study well textilery and act in such a way
That they will recommend you, 'twill help some other day

Dear Junior

I guess you are "sorter" lonesome and we are lonesome too
Since your folks out there left you, guess nothing else would do
I guess you'll make it ok, if careful you will be
Just keep your eyes wide open and surely you can see

Don't get in any trouble no matter what goes on
If you will just be careful, you'll always get along
You ought, above your smoking; also, above your board,
To save up several dollars and put them in your "gourd"

It's alright to make money but you should never waste
It's a sin to blow it there for something just to taste
The girls all want to see you. We'd like to see you too
When you come bring on Arthur. They're crazy 'bout him too

Tom Thomasson

Dear Junior: March 28, 1934

Kings Mountain, NC

We'll soon have Easter Sunday. It's the last day of March
The next day will be Monday, another month will start
You've had a fine vacation. It's been a lot of help
You've made your board and clothing and made it by yourself

It's better than a sentence as many boys can tell
Three months with a prison gang is like that long in hell
You left the boys to loafer the town here all alone
You can tell them all about it, whenever you come home

The girls here wants to see you. You have been gone so long
If you all come in Easter, that won't be very long
Bring Arthur right on with you. I know we'll have some fun
The girls are crazy 'bout him; but he can have but one

Dear Cora: October 10, 1936

T. J. is now repainting the house in which we live
He goes to school each evening, half-time I must give
You know it looks much better with just a little shine
It only takes a little paint and just a little time

The cabin is "ole ivory" with just a little green
That makes the prettiest house I guess you've ever seen
He's now gone to Copper Hill; basketball he must play
Each weekend with his team he must go away

Tonight when he returns he's planned a camping trip
To take his teachers to the shack to stay a little bit
Bring your boys on over before it gets too cold
You can stay along with us 'til Mr. Adams goes

To T. J. Thomasson, Jr.

Your note to me was no surprise;
no doubt your decision is wise
She is good stock, perhaps well bred.
She'll manage you, her hair is red
I'm sending you your last request.
Of course it will be for the best
Another jolt it was indeed.
Now you may get into the lead

I hope to you she will be true
and help you freely to get through
The sea is deep. The world is wide.
It was for you to decide
I do not know and cannot see
just what your outcome all will be
It looks like, though, your hands are full.
But you'll get through if you will pull

The idea now is settle down
and don't attempt to loaf around
Make your honeymoon quite short,
and then to work again resort
I now commit you to her care,
that each the others' joy may share
Now may you look to Him above
for everlasting peace and love

Image 3-4: In this photo, Tom Thomasson is seated. All of his children, with the exception of Floid who died in 1918, are shown. Left to right are Fulton, Zora, T. J., Cora, John Henry and Ora.

Chapter 4

Tom's Family, Part Two

COMMENTARY: Chapter Introduction

Tom Thomasson's children and grandchildren were enumerated at the opening of Chapter Three. He saw many of his great grandchildren into the world as well. The grandchildren and great grandchildren (along with in-laws and other close members of his clan) form the cast of characters in numerous letters, pieces of poetry and post card poems. Examples of those items are included in this chapter.

Mr. Thomasson spent a great amount of time and effort to pass his appreciation for music and literature along to his relations. Many of them took a great concern with such things as well. Mr. Thomasson often got the younger ones together for singing fests and he taught them the particulars of music. He worked with many of his grandchildren, such as Leila, to help them learn to play the pump organ. In *Little Leila* Tom speaks more about her. In between school, play and music lessons Leila faithfully cleaned house for her Granny Thomasson each week. As noted later in the chapter Tom also sponsored a poetry contest for his granddaughters and grand daughters-in-law. Writings entitled *Thanksgiving* and *Mrs. Fay Gregory* provide more details about the contest. Carol Lunsford McCarter, daughter of Ray Lunsford, remembered Tom Thomasson reading poetry to her when she was a child.

Happy adventures of some of Tom's grandsons and great grandsons are set down in tracts such as *Midget, Billy, Just Three Boys* and *T. J. III*. Poems written for granddaughters, apart from those previously mentioned, include *Stella Mae's 16th Birthday*.

Two dirges in this otherwise light-hearted collection are *In Memory of Mother* and *Our Baby, Polly Ann*. The former was written to memorialize the passing of son John Henry's wife, Bennie Mae. The latter work documents the death of newborn Polly Ann Thomasson, daughter of T. J. and Polly Thomasson.

Little Leila

Leila is a pretty little girl with two great big brown eyes
She wears a suit of pretty hair and never loafers 'round
She seldom leavers her mama because she needs her bad
If she does she hurries back, she knows she better had

Of course she forgets sometimes and stays a little late
But when she thinks of the past for others she don't wait
The little folks all like her because she is so kind
And when she gets some candy she makes it go around

Her aims are very lofty. She wants to go through school
She studies well her subjects and never breaks a rule
She gathers up the children; they all like to play school
She is their little teacher and they observe her rules

They all admire their teacher and mind her very well
If not it doesn't differ, not one of them will tell
So when the school is over, each one of them will scat
They know they'll get a lickin' if they don't hurry back

The little teacher hurries. The dishes for her wait
And all the kitchen cleaning, it matters not how late
When the kitchen work is finished, she figures out her plans
For her next day's teaching and where they'll take their stand

Little Leila: "Be pretty if you can. Be witty if you must. Be agreeable if it kills you."

Just Three Boys

I have some little comrades. They're Loster, Charles and James
They are each one full of mischief, but always use their brains
They pull some pranks on David. They devil Billy too
But always get defeated, before they all get through

All boys are very useful to do their little mite
But when you need them badly, they're always out of sight
Some boys are very idle, from duty they will shirk
They often dodge them orders, with other boys to flirt

Too often we rebuke them about their useless toys
Perhaps they'll soon forsake them, but boys are only boys
They all are splendid workers at every job they find
They each one work together and never get behind

They all are strictly honest and do not shun the truth
That makes them all reliable, though each one is a youth
They don't believe in cheating but contend for all their own
I've tested them completely, when we was just alone

Now when I go to pay them, they watch me very close
And if I over pay them, they know it is a joke
They give me back the over-plus. They know it is mine
They realize I'd chase them for at least a full mile

Note: David's identity is not certain. The other boys are grandsons.

J. B. Gregory's Fortieth Birthday

I killed Gregory's rooster, I killed him with a stick
I broke his neck square in two so he could hardly kick
Zora picked up each feather and put them in a pan
To waste a single feather she thinks would be a shame

Some folks says she's stingy, but we know that's not so
She was taught to be saving, most everybody knows
She invited all the neighbors to help eat that big cock
She cooked him nearly all day. He was as tough as a rock

She had a splendid supper. We ate and ate and ate
But after we had eaten, we could hardly sleep
Now don't call folks stingy because they save some scraps
Save all the little feathers and the tobacco sacks

If you will save the pennies, the dollars you'll save too
Just let folks call you stingy if nothing else will do
It means half of the living, just like it's always been
To throw out half your victuals is nothing but a sin

Bobbed Hair

Polly got her hair bobbed. Her ma said 'twas a sin
"You should not have cut your hair. It won't look good again."
Why do preachers cut their hair, the beard shave from their chin
If cutting hair and beard's not wrong, is bobbing hair a sin?

Should preachers let their hair alone, and let their beard grow long
So that they will always look like Peter, James and John?
All girls used to wear long hair, the boys all wore mustache
But fashions now all have changed, with neither one attached

Our Baby, Polly Ann

Baby's gone somewhere above
To join the happy angel band
The one we each so dearly love
Our darling baby, Polly Ann

Why God taken her so soon
We do not fully understand
Her grave is now with flowers strewn
Our darling baby, Polly Ann

Our hearts so sad we cannot tell
It's almost more than we can stand
But God who doeth all things well
Took our darling baby, Polly Ann

Her stay with us was just a space
Down here in this sinful land
God had prepared a better place
For darling baby, Polly Ann

But we will see her, by and by
With that happy Angel Band
Far, far above the stormy skies
We'll be with baby, Polly Ann

Dear Cora: September 10, 1934

You asked us to send some names, just like good names was scarce
A man always makes his name, beginning at his birth
We know the boy must be named; a name is just a sound
He can build, you see, that name or let that name go down

A name does not make a man, but a man makes a name
Just name that boy if you can and let him build his fame
"Thomas Matthew" will not do. Such a name will not shine
There's nothing much to these two; they're always far behind

You know we will neither care, nor raise a bit of kick
The boy will be better off to know none of our tricks
"Gaston" should be the name, the center of the strike
The mills shut down 'till he came to make things go all right

Note: This set of verses was written as a post card poem while Cora Thomasson Lunsford and her family were working at Gastonia NC. In anticipation of the birth of her child, Cora must have queried her family in Andrews for possible names. The child, born at Gastonia in October of 1935, was ultimately named Thomas Matthew Lunsford.

Tommie's First Poem

Written by Sarah Jean (Tommie) Lunsford, Ridgecrest Baptist Assembly, 7/22/1949

Dear Grandpa:

> I have never written poetry
> But at this time I'll try
> I like the Baptist's Ridgecrest
> I'll try to tell you why
>
> First, I guess, are the preachers
> Who ask us to do our best
> Then comes the recreation
> With play and plenty of rest
>
> There are many handsome boys
> At Baptist's Ridgecrest
> But of all that I have found
> I love my grandpa best
>
> I'm using Grandpa's money
> The money that I earned
> I am buying things with it
> At every crook and turn
>
> Now Grandpa can write poetry
> But poor me can only try
> Everybody knows I love Grandpa
> And nobody knows just why

Tommie

T. J. III

I hope this boy is thriving
He's my little grandson
He's now in Alabama
Beneath the scorching sun

This boy is a real dandy
I think he's two years old
He wants to follow daddy
Just everywhere he goes

His head is nearly round
His eyes are both dark blue
His hair is red and curly
His deeds are very true

They have "snaked" him here
They've "snaked" him there
Sometimes it looks to me
They'll snake him everywhere

He is now down in Florence
In "Florence, Alabam'"
A place that is so crowded
Some folks had better scram

Now when that job is over
They'd better bring him home
Where he can be with granddad
And never have to roam

We will have a good old time
But never loaf around
We'll look after our affairs
And build up our own town

Tom Thomasson

We will try to be content
Because we know it's best
We do the things we want to do
And then sit down and rest

The breezes here are extra fine
They beat the Alabam'
If we get a little hot
We'll say "Electric fan, please"

66

Stella Mae's 16th Birthday

Written October 1, 1943

Stella is a splendid girl. We see her every day
And every time we see her, we just see Stella Mae
She is exactly what she is, let things come as they may
For every time you meet her, you just meet Stella Mae

She is very tall and handsome. Her eyes a wee bit gray
We everyone admire her. Her name is Stella Mae
She really is a model and example by the way
For other girls to mimic. Her name is Stella Mae

She never chose to loafer. She wasn't taught that way
She makes her moments useful. Her name is Stella Mae
She is very optimistic, don't idle time away
She's kind to everybody. Her name is Stella Mae

She talks of things ideal. She speaks of things that pay
She really is a genius. Her name is Stella Mae
She worries much about the war. She talks about T. J.
And other boys in service, Her name is Stella Mae

We need a lot of other girls to cheer us on our way
With little deeds of kindness just like Stella Mae
She now is celebrating her sixteenth birthday
A better girl was never born. Still she is Stella Mae

In Memory of Mother

June 10, 1949: For Patricia

Mother's gone, our precious mother
From this Earth we know this true
But we trust someday we'll meet her
In that land beyond the blue

Her kindly voice we do not hear
Her smiles we do not see,
But in our hearts we have no fear
Those lovely smiles will always be

She was so kind and so devoted
God took her from us away
From Earth to Heaven her soul promoted
Where there is one eternal day

We are lonely, Oh! so lonely
Since she went from us away
But we know that we can only
Look to God for help each day

Our hearts are so sad, you know down here
But yours are sadder, we know, up there
But let's submit to God's great will
Because he doeth all things well

We know our circle here is broken
Our hearts are lonely, lonely here
But we trust the promise spoken
Oh! may it not be broken there

Oh! may we, daddy and all her friends
Meet her above this world of sin
With Mother in our arms of love
Where all is joy and peace and love

Billy

Your baby chicks that got away
are doing well I'm glad to say
I'll treat them good, perhaps someday
the cock will crow, the hen will lay

The cock is black, the hen is brown
they left their roost and came back down
They first escaped us in the brush
and then they hid among the grass

We'll plug their teeth and paint their eyes
so other chicks will know they're wise
I guess that they will multiply
and then the stock will sell quiet high

When you come home they'll be your own
to take with you where e'er you roam
Just feed them well on mash and bran
and soon they will stock the whole land

Two Little Comrades

David and Billy are comrades, with many little toys
Each day they play together, two pretty little boys
Sometimes they get confused and make a lot of noise
But we must all remember that they are little boys

Now when their daddies lick them, they take it all as joys
And kindly tell each other "All daddies lick their boys"
I don't like to see them licked because they are good boys
Of course they do some funny tricks; but still they are good boys

These boys will stick together. There's no one knows their joys
They will fight for each other, for they are comrade boys
If you would avoid trouble, don't meddle with their toys
For they will try to lick you, if they are little boys

We must help these little comrades, their pleasures not destroy
And keep in mind exactly just when you were little boys
It doesn't pay to censure whenever they annoy
They'll soon be educated to teach some other boys

Note: "Billy" is Billy Thomasson, Fulton Thomasson's son and Tom Thomasson's grandson. The identity of "David" is unaccountable. He may have been a neighborhood friend and/or a member of one of Tom's tenant families.

Thanksgiving 1957

Dear Granddaughter:

I think you'll like this letter much better than the last
Perhaps you'll place the contents behind a plate of glass
I think we've played the nicest game that we've ever played
I hope you'll be satisfied with the amount you're paid

I like the game of kindness, a game of peace and love
Like the one we've just now played, handed down from above
I'm puzzled just a little bit to know how each one ranks
But I think I've got it figured out with many, many thanks

I'm sure that all contestants did everything they could
If they could have done better I'm sure each one would've
Everyone of my contestants no doubt with me agree
That all should be rewarded as equal as can be

As I am acting sponsor so I must be the judge
Let everyone share equal and let there be no grudge
If you did the best you could, you did all you could do
So one twelfth the grand prize must go right straight to you

I thank you for your efforts; I praise you for your pride
I love you for your goodness; let angels be your guide
I'm sure I did the best I could, 'cause conscience was my guide
Please don't fail to let me know if you are satisfied

Congratulations to the best all 'round girl of my twelve granddaughters in this contest for a $100.00 cash prize.

Your Grandfather, T. J. Thomasson; Andrews, North Carolina

Note: This letter of poetry was sent to Faye Lunsford Gregory in 1957. Tom Thomasson ran a poetry contest for his granddaughters and wives of his grandsons. Since Fay was married to Tom's grandson, J. B. Gregory, she met the qualifications for entry. Also, Faye was the daughter of George Lunsford who married Tom's daughter Ora.

Mrs. Faye Gregory: December 5, 1957

Dear Granddaughter

I hope you all are satisfied and pleased with your reward
In our little contest game and that all are in accord
My granddaughters are my pride; you have all been nice to me
I respect you for your good news as everyone can see

I love you for your kindness, respect you for your pride
Your kisses placed upon my cheeks would never be denied
You answer to my request for your goodness all around
I want everyone to know, will in my heart abound

Your letters now all stack up, I read them o'er and o'er
And every time I read them, I appreciate them more
My granddaughters are my girl friends; they are my twelve in one
Of course they're most of all to me, and they I'll never shun

Merry Xmas and Happy New Year

Love Granddad Thomasson

Midget

Midget is a noble boy. He lives at Valley Town
He does the work all up well and never loafs around
He is a real good fellow, folks can say what they please
He does his work up quickly, and then he rests with ease

He feeds all of the horses and curries all the mules
He ties up all his goaties and then he's off to school
He never waits for Jackie; he says he is too slow
He does like his great-granddad, most everybody knows

When he is writing poems, he does his very best
He counts his words correctly, then rhythm does the rest
He is a real example; this boy you cannot fool
He has up all his lessons, before he gets to school

He tells Jane and Jackie, to learn with all their might
For things that are done by halves are never half done right
He is doing well in school; I'm glad I can tell you
That he seldom ever goes below his P's and Q's

Note: Midget was a childhood nickname for Raymond Carroll (Ray) Gregory who was Tom's Great-grandson. His parents, J. B. and Faye Lunsford Gregory also had children called Jane, Jackie, Stella Ann and Martha. Another daughter, Norma Marie, died at birth.

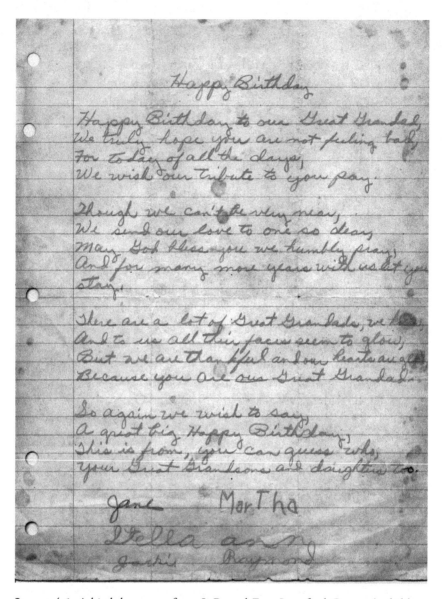

Image 4-1: A birthday poem from J. B. and Faye Lunsford Gregory's children is shown above.

Reply to Jack & Ray Gregory

Hello there my little boys, you nasty old sweet things
You beat me on the poems, as sure as anything
I note you both are coming, soon as the bees all swarm
I hope that they will hurry as sure as you are born

You will have to give them time to leave the old "B" gum
Then you all must hurry up so we can have some fun
I hope they will all be boys; we will call one Stella May
One Tom and one will be Jane, The balance will all be "Faye's"

Your Grand- and Great-granddad Thomasson

Chapter 5

Longtown and "The Town," Part One

COMMENTARY: Chapter Introduction

Many of the details concerning exactly why and when Tom and Exie Thomasson moved their family from the Peachtree Community to Andrews, NC have been consumed by the ages. In some formal writings, it is stated that Tom Thomasson moved to Andrews in 1933. Other records, as well as first hand historical accounts, place members of the family there much earlier. This incongruity may be linked to statements about when Tom moved with his family to his "final homeplace" at Andrews.

None of the Thomassons appear in the 1920 census of Andrews or of nearby settlements. Tom, Exie, Fulton, Cora and T. J. all appear on the 1930 census in a single household. Zora and her husband Bert are nearby as are Ora and her husband George, each with their respective families in separate houses. It is of note that Fulton was studying at Andrews High School in the mid 1920s. The family was a well established presence by the late 1920s.

The various family members lived in at least five separate homes, all in the same neighborhood, during the early years. It is likely that Tom Thomasson took up occupancy in his "final" home at Andrews around 1933. All of this formed the nucleus for what Tom Thomasson would later refer to as "The Town." To help readers understand the fine details, a bit of schooling on history and geography is in order.

Andrews is a town in Cherokee County, NC. The town proper, with its businesses, was slightly less than a mile away from where Tom Thomasson and his family settled. One name for the rural community where Tom and Exie lived is "Longtown." That name has been in use for decades. Before the road running through the community was formally named "Bristol Avenue" many people referred to it by that name (or by "Longtown Road") in both speech and print. A few have called it "Slaughter Pen Road." That name is preserved in at least one old deed from the community.

A number of people still remember the one lane dirt road which was first widened and paved in the early 1970s. Prior to it being graveled, the road was sometimes treated with crushed cinder to improve traction during spells of bad weather. Tom Thomasson's poem *Save the Scraps* describes an ingenious, though environmentally unfriendly, attempt to deal with the dusty road during dry weather. Many people have memories of the tar and gravel mixture used on the road in the late 1970s and 1980s. During hot weather it would melt and stick to shoes. Herman Hardin used to joke that he got two inches taller just by walking home from school. Eddie Lunsford remembered his dad cleaning tar off his school shoes with gasoline and an old shop rag.

Most people assume that Longtown was named for early residents with the last name "Long." Over the course of time a lot of such people lived there. Thomas Finley Long and his wife Mollie V. King Long are mentioned in deeds from the area dated 1908 and 1911. Thomas' brother Leonidas N. Long and his wife, Carrie Glenn Long, conveyed local property to them in 1907. That couple spent time in Texas before settling more permanently in Georgia. Many members of the Long family had roots in Jackson County, NC.

Thomas and Mollie Long were living with their children somewhere near Andrews at least as early as 1900. The Thomas F. Long residence is specifically mentioned in a deed from the Longtown community which is dated 1911. By all accounts Thomas Long was an incredibly interesting, well rounded, well traveled, well read and well educated man. People would seek out his advice and his opinions on world affairs. He was a good carpenter. It is of note that some houses he built, or helped to build, still stand. Long taught school and served as the Justice of the Peace, both at Andrews, for a time. Long's father pursued the same type of work at Jackson County. The extended Long family has stories about Thomas waking up his daughters to witness late-night weddings at the Long family home.

Mollie Long was described by a granddaughter as a "pretty, sweet woman" who loved people. Thomas gifted all his grandchildren with a commemorative bank, shaped like the Liberty Bell, when he visited a world's fair exhibition in the 1920s. The couple later exited the Andrews, NC area and eventually settled in Arizona. They are buried at Maricopa County. Thomas and Mollie left a legacy in Longtown and the surrounding area. One of their sons was named Homer. His wife was Laura Nichols Long. That couple, along with their children, are noted in the 1920 and 1940 census records from the Longtown community. They also had a home closer to the town of Andrews, near the school, during another period of history. Much like his father, Homer was a skilled and thorough carpenter. He was well known and well liked. Another of the Long clan, Bob, lived in the Longtown settlement with his family in the 1960s. He was also remembered as being a good neighbor. The Long daughters, Barbara and Susie, (and their mother Delphia) had many friends.

The boundaries of Longtown are as informal and open to discussion as possible. Since it was never anything close to an organized township, the starting and stopping points are a matter of opinion. Some people insist that Longtown actually begins at the corner of Cherry and Aquone Streets and runs along the road now known as Bristol Avenue to what is today called the "Slaughterpen Curve." That landmark, by the way, got its name honestly. In old days there was a routinely used complex, past the curve, established for the purpose of killing of livestock raised for food. Other people describe Longtown as beginning about a half mile further up the road, nearer to the place along Bristol Avenue where the Brady family (Felix, Zenna, Austin and their descendants) lived for so long. Some have called that "upper Longtown."

There is an interesting history in the community that precedes the Longs. Of course the land that was to become Longtown was used and inhabited by the Cherokees for ages untold. Throughout the region there were a few pioneer families including some parented by mixed Cherokee/European marriages. After the formation of Cherokee County in 1839 a flurry of claimants for land grants appeared out of nowhere. It is very likely that some of these people put claim to land they would never even lay eyes on. Many were driven by greed, hopes for fast cash from timber sales or by anticipation of long-term cash flow supported by mineral royalties. Some men were awarded title to land in later years as a nod to their service during the Civil War.

Nearly all of the land that would become the Longtown community was acquired by Abel Jackson (Ab) Leatherwood, his wife Elvira and their daughter Sarah Adeline (Addie) Leatherwood in the 1800s. They had large property holdings, including a tract of more than 200 acres which had Tatham Creek as one of its boundaries. Some of the Leatherwood property was previously owned by the Lenoir family, famous in eastern Tennessee and western North Carolina. The Leatherwood home site was on the outskirts of the old Valley Town settlement on what is today called "Aquone Street." Many local residents still call that stretch "the Old Mill Road." As of this writing the Leatherwood house (though extensively remodeled and updated in later years) still survives.

In 1900 Addie Leatherwood took ownership of a significant portion of the Leatherwood family land. One of the first things she did was to negotiate a deal with James Taylor Pullium and his wife Myra Martin Pullium for farm/forest acreage in the middle of what would become Longtown. The formalized deal took place at least as early as 1906 with the Pulliums taking full ownership around 1912. Some of the Pullium descendants still own, and reside on, that property.

Not too long after the transaction involving the Pullium family, Addie Leatherwood conveyed a 110 plus acre tract to Dr. Horace N. Wells. The Long property, and others, would be derived from that land. Wells was a physician from the Pigeon Valley region of Haywood County, North Carolina. According to members of his extended family, Dr. Wells was educated at Harvard University. He came into Cherokee County with his wife Laura in the early 1900s, settling for a time in Andrews. From Andrews he lived in Murphy before returning to Haywood County.

Even in Haywood County, Wells demonstrated a propensity toward public service. He had his medical practice, his family; and he dabbled in many community affairs. Once in Cherokee County, he apparently maintained no formal medical practice but focused on other pursuits. His interests were multifaceted and perhaps even contradictory. There can be no doubt that he made money trading real estate. Pages and pages of deeds (spanning decades and coming from practically all over the county) bear his name. Yet he also appeared to be very civic-minded. He was a charter member of the Andrews, NC Board of Aldermen. He served as the town's mayor between about 1909 and 1911. Local historians note that Wells helped to promote town schools and the public library at Andrews.

In 1925 H. N. Wells wrote an editorial for the *Cherokee Scout* newspaper arguing for the establishment of a national park in the Smoky Mountains. The language he selected to describe his love and reverence for nature is breathtaking:

There are those who would love for this part of the state to become historic and noted for its supreme heights, beautiful streams, lovely flowers, clear sky, salubrious air and charming beauty. God has lavished so much primeval beauty and grandeur amid [their] supernal heights we of one accord should combine our efforts to keep it so. The woodman must lay down his axe, the pot hunter and fisher must set aside his gun and rod, and all join with one accord not to invade this land of primitive beauty except to admire and love it; healed by breathing its balsamic odors, drink of its sparkling fountains, and be soothed to rest by the song of birds and the mourn of the winds. I have crossed the continent twice, fished on the beach of the two great oceans and also in the Rockies, but give me the Big Smoky range for the outing and I am content...I have stood upon the summit of the tallest peak of the Great Smoky range just as the gates of day were opened and the first rays of the morning sun gilded these dizzy heights and looked far below when the early morning streams covered the valleys beneath and was enchanted beyond description..."

*****

"The Town" as described by Tom Thomasson in his writing was more intimate and defined than even "upper Longtown." It is of note that Tom Thomasson began to buy, acquire and build a number of houses which he shared among his family and which he rented to various people over the course of time. It is that area of the neighborhood which Tom jokingly referred to as "The Town" or sometimes as "my town." In the next couple of chapters Tom's terminology ("The Town") will be used to refer mostly to "Upper Longtown."

In the past "the Town" was an active and thriving community. Tom Thomasson and his son Fulton never had trouble filling their rental homes. Some of the houses were built entirely from scratch; others utilized outbuildings or other existing structures for their framework. Tom or members of his family did much of the work themselves. Professionals like master mason Wade Pullium would be called upon as their talents were needed. In the 1930s running water was added to most of the houses. Tom's son, T. J., wired the houses for electricity in the 1940s. He was assisted by George Lunsford's son Cecil. "Blast you!" was Tom's response when Cecil tumbled through the ceiling and landed at Tom's feet as he relaxed in front of the fireplace while the wiring was taking place.

In a letter to his granddaughter Stella Mae Gregory in the 1940s, Tom noted with delight that one of his homes was bringing the incredible price of $4.25 per week. On the odd occasion Tom's daughter Ora would rent out a room in her home on a short term basis. Some of Ora and George's children recalled being paid a small sum in coins to carry water each day to a couple renting an upstairs bedroom.

Tenants in the rental properties were varied and many. Some stayed for years, others for mere days or weeks. Some of the rental properties began to fall to disrepair by the early 1970s. As well as can be remembered, the final tenant left the last occupied house on what will shortly be described as "the Wilson property" in the early 1990s. Mr. Ken Grant moved out of Tom Thomasson's home in about 2003. Tom's granddaughter Tommie, and her husband Jerry Bumgarner, used the house as a weekend and vacation retreat after that.

What follows is a list of families (or individual's family names) that lived at and/or owned property in what is now the Longtown community since about the mid 1800s. Of course the list is not complete. No omissions were made deliberately. If a family name is marked with an asterisk (*) more than one family with that name is noted.

Adams   Allison   Ammons

Barton   Beck   Berrong   Best   Bishop   Blevins   Bradley   Brady   Bristol   Bryant   Buchanan   Bumgarner   Burchfield   Burnette

Cassady   Cathey   Chambers*   Childers   Coker   Conley   Cotter   Crawford   Crisp   Cunningham   Cutshaw

Davis   Day   Deitz   Dockery   Dysart

Falkner   Flowers   Frazier   Fulford

Garrett   George   Gibby   Goss   Gragg   Grant*   Gregory*   Gribble   Griffith*   Gruber   Guffey

Hardin* Harris Head Hedden* Hensley Henson Hicks* Hill
Hogan* Hogsed Holland Horn* Huffman Hughes Hyde

Johnson Jones*

Kristofferson

Lambert Leatherwood Ledford Lee* Lenoir Lequire Long*
Love Lovingood Lunsford*

Maennlee Mashburn* Matheson* McClain McClelland Mintz
Moore* Morton Mosteller Muncey

Neal Nelson Nichols* Nicholson* Norris

Palmer Parker Postell Powers Pullium*

Raxter Reece Robinson Rogers* Rowland

Samuels Sanchez Smith Stevens Stillwell Summner

Thomasson* Thompson Twiggs

Waldroup Wells West* Whitaker White* Wilson Wooten Wyke

Young

Just a Stroll: 1934

We strolled out Easter Sunday
Three good pets and me
Wilma, Faye and Stella Mae
To see what we could see

We went away up the road
About the Bristol gap
We strolled all o'er the hills
Before we started back

Now this was Easter Sunday
Nineteen and thirty-four
We had a good vacation
If we don't have no more

Grandpa put out some big words
We couldn't hardly crack
Wilma said she'd get the hammer
As soon as she gets back

One word was "magnificent"
I never heard that beat
Then Faye said "Hallelujah
Whoopee sir," she said "you poet."

We gathered some toothbrushes
To use for souvenirs
When we passed the slaughter pen
We had to hold our ears

We may stroll again someday
We had such a nice time
Then we will make some poems
And every one will rhyme

Note: Wilma and Faye were sisters. They were the daughters of George W. Lunsford who was married to Tom's daughter Ora. Faye married Tom's grandson, J. B. Gregory. His sister was Stella Mae. The "toothbrushes" they gathered were likely twigs from a black gum tree. During the walk, "Grandpa" (Tom Thomasson) apparently held a spelling bee.

Save the Scraps

The motor oil they saved
All come in mighty nice
Although it had been used
Now it has been used twice

We high-toned the station lad
Because it was a waste
He freely gave it to us
To save a little space

We smeared it well on the street
In front of our new house
That oil now has helped a lot
We used it every ounce

That oil of which we speak
Has surely done its part
For many miles it greased the wheels
Of the old motor car

When you can improve your street
Without one cent of cost
It sure is very very nice
When no one suffers loss

Our street is nice and greasy now
The dust is lying low
We get out without sneezing
When e'er we wish to go

From steps to steps between us all
The street looks mighty good
We could have fixed it sooner
If just we only would

You know it pleases our neighbors
To get rid of the dust
For each one of them contended
That their dust was the worst

If you will be economic
The oil change to save
And spread it on all our streets
We'll soon see that it pays

Thanksgiving

We are thankful for our rock wall
(With many other things).
The wall is built the crazy way
with many curves and rings

You all must come and see it
We finished it today
The stones are placed so perfect
I'm sure that they will stay

This being Thanksgiving Day
it cost one and one-half time
But I'm sure it's worth the cost
it took most of my dimes

I know I don't begrudge them
the bank's out of the way
And those rough rocks are shining
I see them every day

It contains two flights of steps
as nice as they can be
A sign midway between them:
"To rent a house – see me"

Among the jobs completed
in all the recent past
I am sure that this rock wall
is showing up the best

I'm getting a kick out of my wall
as everybody knoweth
But I must bloweth my own horn
or it won't be blowethed

Mrs. Thomasson's (Mom's) Flower Garden

I'm watching now, Ma's flowers grow
She says, "Those flowers you must test."
I said, "It's too much for me to say
when nature does her best."

I'm watching now her flowers bloom
As I have watched before
It looks to each one, the other tries
To bloom a little more

Each flower has its own task
And tries to do its best
It has a lot of work to do
If it beats all the rest

I'm still watching Ma's plants grow
I see her flowers bloom
Each one seems to say to me
Now which one will you choose?

The garden now is over flown
With many colors bright
Gladiolus take the lead I guess
But most of them are white

The larkspur and the daisies
Are standing all upright
With nature's decorations
It is a pretty sight

Each flower has its own name
As other things has got
The most appropriate name, I guess,
Is that of "touch me not"

Each plant has its natural form
And its peculiar bloom
With all the colors and designs
And many sweet perfumes

The question now is to decide
And satisfy our sight
A question we cannot decide
When nature fixed them right

Joseph's coat without a bloom
But foliage so grand
Shows nature's wonderful love
And nature's own great plans

Nature's flowers are all great
But Joseph's coat is grand
Without a flower on that coat
For that coat – I must stand!

Dear Cora: September 3, 1934

Those flowers still are growing and blooming by the way
There's no one here that's knowing how long here they will stay
The nights are growing chilly. The frost is getting near
To make those flowers wither and kill them we all fear

We're trying hard to keep them until you all come home
So that you all can see them and we won't be alone
Some are green and some are gray, along the rustic wall
We spray them good every day, to moisten up the soil

So now if we don't keep them, it won't be our fault
Into the house we'll take them before there comes a frost
We want you all to see them before they all are dead
We'll do our best to keep them, for they are meat and bread

Dear Cora: September 9, 1934

Those flowers still are blooming, along our rustic wall
The honey bees are sipping the honey from them all
The hummingbirds attend them to make them more complete
They are humming and humming the honey bees to beat

It surely is the odor; attracts those birds and bees
They surely find each other and find it at their ease
The crickets now are chirruping beneath our rustic wall
They say that frost is coming to kill our flowers all

We wish that we could keep them along through all the year
If providence would let us, because they are so dear
But nature makes them wither and causes them to die
Just like He does his people, He takes above the sky

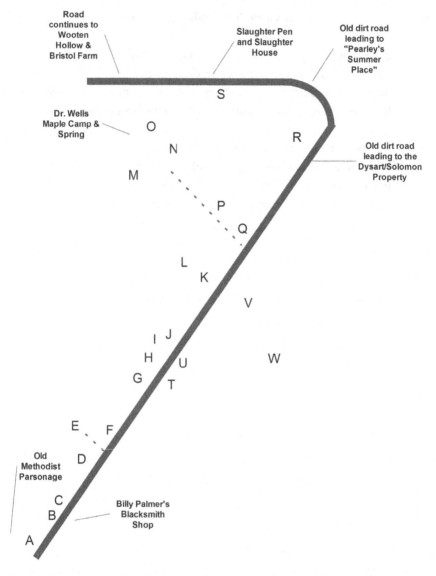

Image 5-1: Map of the Longtown Community, circa 1940s to early 1970s. Houses are identified by letters of the alphabet and will be referenced in the text to follow. Members of the Thomasson and/or Lunsford families had ownership of houses C, G, H, I, J, K, L, M, N, P, Q, R, T, U, V and W at various points in time. Image created with Edraw Max.

COMMENTARY: Tour of Longtown

This section will offer a tour of Tom Thomasson's "town" as well as of the Longtown community. One could journey along the route and encounter at least 20 houses during The Town's heyday. What follows is a tour of that area across time. Readers are asked to accept apologies, in advance, for the poor quality of the few photographs which could be located and copied. The photos are offered as landmarks in time to assist readers. To begin the tour, imagine that you are walking from Main Street in Andrews, NC toward and through Longtown, along what is today called "Bristol Avenue." As you walk, reference the beginning of the tour with the houses on the left-hand side of the road. The tour will begin with house A, noted at the lower left corner of the map shown in Image 5-1. Perhaps you will be joined on your imaginary tour by Tippy Palmer (Image 5-2).

Image 5-2: Tippy Palmer surveys Longtown Road from his perch on a retaining wall. Note the Bristol pasture across the road. The stack of lumber came, perhaps, from the Bristol mill.

The property upon which house A now sits (there was an older house there previously) is widely known today as the "Brady property." Felix Brady and his wife Zenna occupied the home site for many years and added to their property holdings over time. Zenna Lunsford Brady was a grandniece of Neil, Lawson and George Lunsford who will all be discussed shortly. Prior owners of the Brady land included various members of the Matheson family (J. B., Ray, Mel and others). Dr. Wells and the Leatherwoods were earlier owners of at least 22 acres of the Matheson property as evidenced by a deed dated 1907. In a deed from 1911, M. S. (Mel) Matheson and his wife Gussie conveyed a 50 X 200 foot lot to W. T. (Billy) Palmer. A description of the property from the deed notes the lot as "Being the land on which Palmer is now erecting a house." Some details of the house B are shown in Images 5-3 and 5-4. The Palmers were early settlers of the community. Mrs. Palmer (nee Sarah Hicks) was remembered by relatives and former neighbors as an excellent cook.

The Palmers added to, and improved, their property over time. In later years, with the help of son Gene, a beautiful set of stone steps and a retaining wall were added. Some of that detail is shown in Image 5-4. The retaining wall beside the main road is shown in Image 5-5. Children who lived past the Palmer place often walked along the top of the wall on their way to school.

A Palmer Granddaughter, Betty, remembered living at Longtown with her grandparents in house B. One item that sticks out in her mind relates to the social climate of the World War II era. Betty remembered the family, like so many others across the nation, participating in "war drills." During the exercise, oil lamps had to be extinguished. Even the fireplace was covered with a blanket to block signs of light from outside.

Image 5-3: House B. Refer to Image 5-4 for additional details of the home.

Image 5-4: Some details of house B are shown in a collage. At top left is Billy Palmer and son Paul (Bud). Top right: Sarah Palmer holding Gail Palmer. Ruth Palmer is shown holding a doll. At the bottom is Ruth Wilson Palmer.

Image 5-5: Raymond, Martha and Gail Palmer play along the rock retaining wall.

In summary, the Palmers prospered in Longtown for many years. They lived there until a combination of unusual economic issues necessitated their move to the nearby Happytop community. The Palmer lot was eventually absorbed into the Brady estate.

Image 5-6: Grandson Raymond Palmer out for a ride under the supervision of Billy.

House C is the first house in the tour which Tom Thomasson owned. He acquired ownership of the house and three accompanying small tracts of land between 1932 and 1935. Matheson, Lovingood and Hicks were among the previous owners. Tom rented the house to various tenants over the years. Tom gave the property to his daughter Zora. She, her husband Bert and daughter Stella Mae Gregory were the last residents to live there. Moving up the road (and referring to Image 5-1) note that Bruce Bristol's pasture mostly occupied the space on the right-hand side of the road.

Image 5-7: Five generations of the Gregory family pose on the stone steps leading to the entrance of house C. Thomasson descendant J. B. Gregory with his daughter Jane and grandson Johnny Ray Bryson are shown on the back row. J. B. Gregory's father Bert and Bert's mother Emma Jones Gregory are shown at front.

Image 5-8: A view "down the road" from Ora Thomasson Lunsford's back yard dating from the 1950s or 1960s. In the distance, near the trees at left is house C. In about the center of the photograph is house T with the complete chimney shown. Just barely visible above the roofline of that house is house D. The smaller dwelling at the top, right is house G. At the extreme right, barely visible through heavy vegetation is house U. Some outbuildings are shown behind that house.

House D was often called the "old Chambers place." George William (G. W.) Chambers lived there as did other members of his extended family over the course of time. It is believed that G. W. Chambers built the house just prior to 1910. His family was from eastern Tennessee. He was married to Adeline Hicks.

Mr. Chambers purchased the property upon which house D sat from the Mathesons who, in turn, had obtained it from Dr. Wells. Many members of the Chambers family lived in Longtown and significantly figured in to its history. For example, Mr. Chambers' son Ralph Q. Chambers married the youngest daughter of J. T. Pullium. Her name was Ocie. A niece of Mr. Chambers, Sarah Hicks, married Billy Palmer. Some of the details relevant to them and other Chambers descendents are discussed elsewhere in this writing.

Image 5-9: Matheson grandson Jimmy Collins stands at an interesting spot along the tour of Longtown. Note the small barn in the Bristol pasture next to Jimmy's right shoulder. Behind and to his left was what is today called "Chambers Lane." House D would have sat on the hill behind that. The Matheson house, house F. would have been to the right on the image.

Immediately past house D was a dirt driveway. It was officially named "Chambers Lane" in the recent past (see Image 5-9). That road led into a hollow to another small house, "house E." Early owners of that property included W. L. Matheson, Dr. H. N. Wells, C. H. and Martha West, J. W. Horn as well as members of the Robinson family. Many owners and renters occupied the property through time. Family names include Conley, Hensley, Hicks, Dysart, Stevens, White and Hughes. In her 2005 book, *Gratitude for Shoes*, Cleo Hicks Williams shared memories of house E dating from the early 1950s when she lived there with her brother I. M. (Sweetie) Hicks and his wife Ruth. Williams noted the house sat on a slope along one side of the hollow. The following is from p. 305 of Williams' book:

Ruth and Sweetie lived on Slaughter Pen Road, about a mile from town. The paved street, cracked sidewalk and far spaced street lights ended at the park, just a little ways off Main Street up the road toward their house. They lived back out of site in a holler, on a routed-out dirt road. A car could usually make it in and out all right, but after a rain it was too slick to risk sliding off into a rut and getting stuck or damaging a car...They had a living room, kitchen and two bedrooms, with a full length porch and a smaller back porch where the wringer washer sat. The spring was down a little trail behind the house. They had a nice big garden on the hill above the house.

The Neil Lunsford family once lived in house E as well. They eventually settled in house R, to be discussed later. Miss Catharine Serene Morton, a well respected school teacher in Andrews, lived in house E and the pretty hollow for years. Image 5-10 shows a portion of her yard.

Image 5-10: A portion of Miss Catharine Morton's yard was captured in this photo. Beautiful flower beds and some of Morton's animal cages are shown. House E would have been situated to the right of the images shown in the photo.

House F would be encountered as one walked out of the hollow from House E. In other words, if you stood at the intersection of what are today Bristol Avenue and Chambers Lane, house D would have been to your left, house F to your right and house E in the hollow into which Chambers Lane leads. Images 5-1 and 5-9 can assist in clarifying those spatial relationships.

The Matheson family, along with the Pulliums, Palmers and Longs, were some of the earliest settlers of the community. House F was occupied by William L. (Will) Matheson who purchased his property directly from Dr. Wells in 1912. The deed makes mention of it "being part of Leatherwood tracts..." Mr. Will Matheson was remembered as a skilled woodworker and carpenter. House F was very ornate in its construction with much attention to detail. It was also a very solidly built structure.

With his wives, Julia and Mattie, Will Matheson had a large family. Within the list of relatives may be found another Longtown familial connection. Will's daughter Vinnie married Dallas (Rosco) Hicks, a relative of Sarah Hicks Palmer. Following the death of Mattie Matheson, the house sat empty for a few years before being lost in a fire in the 1970s. Image 5-11 shows some details of house F.

Image 5-11: A collage of Matheson family photos showing details of the structure of house F. Mattie Lovingood Matheson is shown at the top-right with family members Ruth, Bobby, Tommy and Bob. She is also pictured along the bottom-middle with two grandchildren. Daughter Vina is bottom-left. Granddaughter Kathy is show at extreme right, top and bottom.

Past the Matheson place (house F) on the left, one would have encountered house G high on the brow of the hill. It was a tiny rental house built by Tom Thomasson. Its construction is documented in the poem *Dear Stella Mae*. There was a beautiful and massive set of stone steps, with high walls, that led to the tiny dwelling. At the time the house was put together, Cecil Lunsford would have been around 12 years old. He told that his first paying job was to straighten recycled nails for the project. He was paid one nickel per hour for his work. Cecil labored on the task while sitting at another set of stone steps nearby. Ownership of house G was transferred to Tom's descendants. Today the property is owned by members of the Lunsford family.

Houses T and U represent two "home places" occupied by Tom and Exie Thomasson near Andrews, NC. On our imaginary tour, those houses would be situated on the right-hand side of the road. In Image 5-8 house T is clearly visible from behind. The property was bought by Tom Thomasson in 1923. G. K. Robinson and his wife Bertha, along with C. H. West and his wife Martha sold the property to the Thomassons. A previous owner was J. W. Best. The Robinsons and Thomassons may have shared a connection from the Peachtree Community. It was house T into which Tom first moved with his family in the 1920s. They appear to have lived there until the early 1930s when house U was completed. After Tom, Exie and their family exited house T it was used as a rental property. For a time, Tom's daughter Zora and her family lived there. When a large family was not living in house T, it could be divided to form two rentals, one downstairs and one upstairs. A running joke about house T was that people sitting on the front stoop had to pull their feet back if a car passed along the road. The front entry of house T was very close to the main road.

House U is what most people will remember as Tom Thomasson's home place. It is barely visible at the extreme right in Image 5-8 due to obstruction by vegetation. Image 5-12 shows the back of the house more completely but it is in poor focus. After Exie Thomasson's death, her daughter Cora came to live in the house and help take care of Tom. Tom's country store (to be discussed in Chapter 6) was quartered mostly in house U. From the time Tom moved in, until the early 2000s, the house underwent various remodels and additions. A basement apartment was frequently rented. During a housing shortage in the early 1940s, a female tenant slept on a cot in a separate single basement room for several days until she was able to find better accommodations. It was during this era that construction projects in the region, including the building of the Nantahala Dam, made housing such a scarce commodity. Referring again to Image 5-8, note that there are two "out buildings" behind house U. These are not described or numbered. It is of note that the property upon which houses T and U were built was originally part of the Long-Lunsford tract.

Image 5-12: House U from behind. In addition to traditional basement space, there was a finished apartment and a small finished basement room.

On another portion of the original Long-Lunsford property in "The Town" a number of houses came and went through time. On the left-hand side of the road was about one acre which was conveyed to J. C. and Addie Crisp in 1907. That property eventually became the W. O. Wilson property and was acquired by Tom Thomasson in 1939.

Image 5-13: A view of most of the "Wilson property" from the early 1970s. Houses G, H and I are shown.

House G was shown in Image 5-8 and has been previously discussed. It is barely visible in the extreme left of Image 5-13. The next house, H, was the Wilson homestead. It was lost in a fire in the early 1970s. The Hardin family later lived in a mobile home at that spot. House I was one of the last occupied rental houses of "The Town." The final tenant moved out in the early 1990s. Prior to the photograph, house I sat at a moderately higher elevation. After some landscaping by heavy equipment, Fulton Thomasson (Tom's son) lowered house I to the location shown in the photo using a wheelbarrow and a shovel. Image 5-14 may also be referenced for some of the structures discussed above.

Image 5-14: This photo was taken in the yard of house V, of which a small portion may be seen at the extreme left. House U is shown toward the center and house H at right. Pullium descendant Hildred Jones Lunsford is shown with two of her children, Dale and Naomi.

Image 5-15: A part of House J is shown enlarged from the background of a group photo. Jack Lunsford and a nephew, Junior Mason, are shown in the foreground.

House J was often known as the "Best House." It sat to the right of house I but higher on the hill. Carlee Best and her husband Sam lived there in the early years. She was a Wilson daughter. Tom wrote about the house, and a set of tenants, in *The White Cabin*. A portion of House J was incidentally caught in a Lunsford family photograph from the 1940s. That is shown in Figure 5-15. Along much of the Wilson place was a rock retaining wall. Its construction was documented in the poem titled *Thanksgiving*.

Image 5-16: The "To Rent a House – See Me" sign was always positioned at the large rock on the retaining wall described in the poem *Thanksgiving*.

The tour of Longtown will now continue across the road. For reference, the properties of discussion sit on the right-hand side of the road, past Tom

Thomasson's home place, house U. The bulk of these properties were conveyed to the Long family by Dr. Wells. Lawson Nicholas Lunsford and his wife Dorcas took ownership of most of it around 1911. Dorcas' sister was Mattie Lovingood Matheson, previously discussed in the context of House F.

By the spring of 1913 Lawson exited the area for the Peachtree community. He transferred ownership of his primary property (as well as another tract, to be discussed later) to recently widowed Lucy A. Nicholson (later Lucy Berrong Dickey). In subsequent years she deeded the properties among three of her children. A son was named Luther. Along with a daughter, Rosa Twiggs, (and another daughter Martha Gragg) they all held deeds to the properties for a span of time. Eventually members of the Lunsford family were able to recover title to all that land. One tract took 80 years to reclaim.

Almost directly behind house U, and being part of the Long-Lunsford portion, was what a few may remember as the "Barton place" including house W. That house is shown in Image 5-17, thought to be the only photo of the dwelling. The shot dates from about 1927. House W was likely a very old structure, probably predating even the Longs and the Wellses. It may have been the first Long family home at Longtown for a short period of time. There is reason to believe that Dr. H. N. Wells may have occupied the house briefly in the early 1900s. He is said to have had a home on what is now Main Street in Andrews. He may also have lived in house V.

Ben Barton lived in house W with his wife Cora Thompson Barton in later years. As well as is known, they were the final occupants. Cora Barton was a niece to Lawson Lunsford, and his brother George, who later acquired that property and others in the community. A deep well was situated near house W. Children playing in the Lunsford pasture were always cautioned about the well. Ruins of house W were demolished in the 1940s.

Image 5-17: Note the well housing at the far right of this photo of house W. The house's old fashioned puncheon floors are clearly visible as well. Lunsford relative Cora Thompson Barton is sitting; holding baby J. B. Daughters Lola and Cleo are shown to the right, along with older son "Buzz."

House V is shown in Image 5-18. It was built by Thomas F. Long in 1900. Lawson Lunsford and his wife Dorcas lived in house V after they acquired it from the Longs. By 1925 Lawson's brother George and his wife Conie moved there. As noted previously, Tom Thomasson's daughter Ora married George Lunsford in 1929. She continued living in the house until it was lost in a fire.

Image 5-18: House V. The image likely dates from the middle 1970s.

Across the road from houses V and W the tour of Longtown will continue. The land had some confusing title changes through time. Readers may recall that the property under discussion was passed to James Taylor Pullium by Addie Leatherwood. In early 1914 James Taylor Pullium made a conveyance of approximately five of his acres to Larkin C. Nichols and wife Eliza Jane Sharp. Pullium noted that the transfer included "my field" on the property description. Three Nichols daughters are noted heavily in Longtown history. Chesstina Nichols married Avery Pullium who was James Taylor Pullium's son. They lived for a time in the community as well. Another daughter, Laura, married Homer Long who was the son of Thomas and Mollie. Emma (often called "Emmer") was a third daughter. She married Frances (France) Adams. They eventually took ownership of the property now under discussion.

The Nichols family constructed what many have called the most beautiful house in Longtown (House K). It was a two story affair with a partially enclosed upstairs portico. Two additional rooms were added downstairs in later years. France and Emmer Adams lived in the house during their time of ownership. The house was intermittently rented and had some surprising uses through time. Those will be discussed in Chapter 6. Image 5-19 shows a rear view of house K.

Image 5-19: Houses K and L shortly before their demolition.

In 1930 members of the Thomasson family took ownership of house K and the surrounding property. Brother and sister Zora and Fulton (with their spouses) acquired the property from France and Emmer Adams. In time, Fulton and his wife Leila took complete ownership. They eventually made the house their permanent residence when their careers as educators landed them in Andrews. When the couple retired to Georgia with one of their sons in the late 1970s the house was rented a couple of times. Behind house K was a structure akin to a combination woodshed and springhouse. Water was piped into the structure at one time to form a cooling box for perishable food. Just as his father had done with the old Wilson woodshed, Fulton repurposed that structure as a small rental house. That house (identified as L) sat behind house K as shown in Image 5-19. It was eventually enlarged and partially surfaced with fieldstone. House L was one of the last houses of the Thomassons' in use by tenants. The final occupants left in the early 1990s.

Fulton Thomasson further added to "The Town" with two more rental houses. Those houses, designated P and Q, were situated across the field from houses K and L. Another way to envision this is as follows. The photographer for Image 5-19 was standing with his back to houses P and Q. Image 5-20, of poor quality, documents those structures.

Image 5-20: Houses P and Q, owned by Tom Thomasson's son Fulton and used as rental properties. The houses were in grave disrepair at the time of the photograph.

Image 5-20 does not do justice to house P shown at the left. Many people have remarked on the beautiful architecture of the two bedroom dwelling. It was covered with fieldstone. The house featured an arched entry with columns at the summit of exterior stone steps. Another striking feature was a basement level garage with a set of interior concrete steps leading to the main floor. The original lessee was Wade Lunsford.

Directly in front of houses P and Q in Image 5-20, readers will notice a small road. We must take that road to continue the tour of Longtown. To clarify the spatial relationships, imagine that we are again walking on Bristol Avenue. House K is to our left and house V to our right. A few yards past house K is a dirt road on the left. It was originally constructed as a wagon road by Dr. Wells and James Taylor Pullium. Dr. Wells, in fact, paid the Pulliums and Addie Leatherwood $15.00 for the right of way to some of his property in 1907. If we walk up that road we can then see houses P and Q to our right. The road takes us to the remainder of the James Taylor Pullium property. Prior to the construction of the Wells/Pullium wagon road, the Pullium property was accessed by way of an older road that began to the left of where house K would be built. That road stretched along the boundary of the Pullium property and ended in the hollow above.

House N (see Image 5-21) was a three room abode occupied by James Taylor Pullium in the early years. He eventually traded the home to George

Lunsford and his wife Conie. The couple lived there for several years before moving to house V. They maintained ownership of house N. Eventually it went to their son Cecil. House N was extensively rented through the course of time. Many Thomasson and Lunsford family members lived there as well. The final lodgers of house N, Shelby Mason Day and her family, domiciled there in the early 1970s. She was a granddaughter of George Lunsford. House M, not shown, was built by the Cecil Lunsford family in the late 1960s.

Image 5-21: Thomasson and Lunsford descendants pose alongside house N. Tom's daughter Zora is shown with her son J. B. Gregory. His children Jane, Jackie and Raymond are also in the photo.

Joining James Taylor Pullium's land was another 11 to 12 acre portion that is of interest. No house is known to have occupied the property. Dr. Wells had the place for a time, as did Thomas Long. Zebulon Vance Sumner and his wife Eva bought the place from the Longs. They in turn passed it to Thomas Jefferson and Hattie Hill.

In reminiscence about T. J. Hill of Murphy, NC his granddaughter noted that Mr. Hill often invested in rural land to turn for a profit. She related that he was especially fond of challenging, rustic farm sites which he would work diligently as garden space. What later came to be known as the "Hill and Bradley tract" would certainly qualify but it is unknown if "Lawyer Tom Hill" ever put in a crop. He held the land for approximately eight years before selling it to W. M. Bradley and his wife Lillie. It was eventually acquired by George and Conie Lunsford, left to woodland and absorbed into the Lunsford estate.

If our tour continued up the dirt road mentioned above, behind house N, we would end in a hollow where various structures have existed through time. They will all be collectively identified as "house O." The nucleus of the property was "Doctor Wells Maple Camp Place and Spring." Its significance will be discussed later. It is noteworthy at this juncture that this was one of the last pieces of property at Longtown which Dr. Wells relinquished. Avery Pullium (son of James Taylor Pullium) owned it for a while as did Lawson Lunsford and R. F. Mashburn. Luther Nicholson and his wife Evelyn Russell Nicholson eventually sold the property to J. D. Harris and his wife. A second parcel, acquired from the Rogers/McClelland properties formed the balance of what came to be known as the "Harris Place." A log cabin is mentioned on a deed from the early 1900s. It was left behind by Dr. Wells. In due course the Harris family had a larger house on the land. In the 1960s, Harris descendants lived in two mobile homes on the property. The land was very briefly rented for camper trailers many years after the Harris descendants had vacated. In time, the Harris tract was incorporated into the Lunsford property.

We are nearing the end of our tour of Longtown. We will exit via the old Wells/Pullium wagon road and return to Bristol Avenue. We will leave behind houses K, L, M, N O, P and Q. As we are about to step onto Bristol Avenue we will turn left to see another attraction on the tour, house R. Image 5-22 shows the tidy dwelling. The acre of Long-Lunsford property upon which the house sat was bisected by Bristol Avenue as the Longtown community grew. Significant to the history of this house and property is the fact that three Lunsford brothers (Lawson, George and Neil) all had ownership of the property over the course of time. In a trade with James Taylor Pullium, George Lunsford swapped this property for house N and its surrounding land. Pullium's daughter Ocie and her husband Ralph Chambers lived in house R, as did the Bill Holland family. At this stage, it is of note that Ocie Pullium Chambers also lived in house D later in her life.

Image 5-22: House R. To the right of the image, along Bristol Avenue, would be "Slaughter Pen Curve."

Our tour of Longtown will soon come to an end as we walk past house R, to our left. The infamous "Slaughter Pen Curve" of Bristol Avenue is the next landmark we pass. To our right is a long, steep, winding dirt road leading into the woods. Those in the know will easily make the connection to this road and the poem called *Pearly's Summer Home*. Tom Thomasson noted that "a driveway then was quickly fixed" in anticipation of the house which was never built. Neil Lunsford often told the story of seeing "more money than I'd ever seen in my whole life" as he witnessed a cash transaction involving a right-of-way leading to the property. A few people still call a portion of this former Matheson property "Dysart Hollow."

Looking directly ahead from Bristol Avenue we would find "Slaughter Pen Gap" leading to the "Bristol Straight" and "Wooten Hollow." Immediately ahead and to our left would be the Hogan property and house S. The property under consideration was formerly part of the Bristol farm. Rush Cutshaw acquired the land in the early 1950s. Later in the decade Everett and Emma Hogan settled there. Some details of the original house are shown in Image 5-23.

Image 5-23: Everett (Dick) and Emma Hogan, along with their sons Bobby and Russell are shown in a collage of photos providing some detail of House S. The house shown was replaced by a more modern one in the 1960s.

Dear Cora: October 20, 1936

T. J.'s got the house painted on the outside and the in
You can see yourself plainly, as often as you grin
We just brought the chimney in, right square into my room
So that I can chew and spit as happy as a coon

Wade Pullium built the chimney. He did it might quick
He made a pretty grate in it. He did it all with brick
He laid a pretty mantle, as cute as it could be
I showed him how to do it, so that it would suit me

My girls brought in flowers, including Carlee West
Nearly every girl in Longtown, except Mrs. Carlee Best
They lined my mantle solid with purple, blue and green
It was the cutest mantle I know I've ever seen

Tom Thomasson

The Cotter Family

The Cotters are our neighbors
Beneath the maple tree
They seem to be as happy
As any two could be

They are a model couple
With model children three
That makes a happy family
Beneath the maple tree

We thank the Cotter family
For efforts they have made
To make their home look better
About the maple shade

We compliment the Cotters
Real progress they have made
While living in our midst
About the maple shade

They each one make us happy
With something kind to say
Tom is optimistic
And so is Edna May

We like to hear them clatter
Especially Robert Hugh
Along with cunning Margaret Ann
No less of Wanda too

They scatter beams of sunshine
Most everywhere they go
That makes us all feel happy
We each one surely know

Of course we're only human
In the Bible we are taught
That no one here is perfect
We each one have our faults

We cannot see the future
And do not understand
But we hope we'll all be happy
Beyond this sinful land

Our Native Pine Cabin:
For Jane and Benny

I'll tell you of our cabin
In these simple little rhymes
It's just above the Cotters
Among the native pines

The rooms are small but cozy
And dressed up very fine
It's just a little cottage
Among the native pines

It cost me lots of money
But I guess you know it's mine
I know you'd like to see it
Among the native pines

The ones who occupy it
Are each so nice and kind
They're Norris and his madam
Among the native pines

They prize the cabin highly
They're jovial all the time
They surely are our neighbors
Among the native pines

We think there is none better
Their lives will ever shine
Of course it's Jane and Benny
Among the native pines

We know there is no other
More cheerful or sublime
To take their welcome places
Among the native pines

Dear Cora: September 20, 1936

We have got the water, the water and the sink
Right in our little kitchen. What have you got to think?
You ought to see your mama. She's tickled now p-green
She steps about politely, like she was sweet sixteen

I am tickled "sorter" too. For me no more she squalls
The "spickets" are so handy. No "Water Jack" she calls
We have all got in "spickets", including Carlee West
Every one along the line, except Mrs. Carlee Best

We got the Lunsford's big spring, and brought it o'er the hill
It gives us water plenty, with water still to spill
We do not use a cutoff. Good water is too free
When you read this poem, you can plainly see

Note: In this composition, and in the next two, Tom Thomasson chronicles for his daughter Cora a major event in The Town. Cora and her family were working away from home in some of the mills at Gastonia. There is a story that Fulton Thomasson crouched at an upstairs window (see Image 5-19, house K) and sighted the Lunsford spring down the barrel of his gun to make sure there was a clear path for the unforgiving lengths of iron pipe that were used to bring water out of the hollow. That distance alone was at least a hundred yards. Fulton dug most of the trenches single-handed with a shovel and a mattock. Some people remember him working in a trench that was above his head as he made improvements on the initial system in later years. In the local vernacular "tickled" means pleased while "sorter" means "sort of." Spigots were called "spickets."

Dear Cora: September 28, 1936

Our "spickets" are still flowing. They're flusher every day
They give us water plenty, with lots to run away
We use the water freely, because we call it ours
So when we get our washings out, we water all our flowers

We do not stop to worry, about a water rent
Don't' call upon your neighbors, nor pay a single cent
Your mamma looks much younger, more prissy every day
She gets around more quickly than before her hair turned gray

She does not call for water, no "Water Jack" at all
But stove wood is so common, for me she often squalls
If I just had a spicket, that would bring in stove wood
You'd know I'd be tickled. I'd make one if I could

Dear Cora: October 1, 1936

Our spickets are now complete. They fit the standard house
We use them when we're scrubbing, most every neighbor knows
Our water pipe is buried, way down 'neath the clay
To keep the water good and cold. We use it every day

The water job is over. The spickets are complete
The water runs every night, to sing us all to sleep
I hope you'll soon be moving, if you all think it's best
You can stay along with us, as well as all the rest

Your house will soon be vacant, by the first of the year
Of course you then can have it, without a doubt of fear
I've wrote you several poems, explaining everything
You surely did not get them. You haven't wrote a thing

COMMENTARY: Front Porch Lore

The following section of this chapter includes some of the stories that would be told and listened to on long summer evenings. After the work was done, and the heat of the day began to fade, it was common practice to gather on the porch before bedtime. Oak-splint bottomed chairs were often full so a few members of the audience would find a resting place on porch steps, against the outside walls or even stretched out on porch rails. Often the younger children would be busy catching lightening bugs in the twilight. If it was a weekend evening, perhaps they would continue their quests even later. When the time of year was right, katydids would sing all night long. Topics of conversation on the front porch were varied. The people and events of the past often provided a lot of fodder for talk. Then as now, some stories were better remembered than others.

A lot of story-worthy events took place at Longtown over the years. There were lots of fun times and interesting events. A good ghost story was always welcome. The most brilliant of all chroniclers of ghostly things was Mattie Bell Hogan Lunsford, often called "Maw" or "Aunt Jenny" by people in the community.

A number of stories from Longtown involved great personal tragedies, untimely deaths and other sad events. Many of these will not be repeated in the interest of protecting living individuals or their immediate families from unwelcome attention. In other cases, names will not be provided in the stories. It is of note that one man who grew up on Longtown, and who did not wish to be identified, said that his childhood there was generally very unhappy. He did have some stories of good times to share.

Image 5-24: Billy Palmer and various members of the Matheson family meet for some whittling and story-telling.

*****

According to the Cherokee Indians the oldest inhabitants of the region are the Yunwi Tsunsdi which came to be called the "Little People." These beings are about two feet tall and have a number of special powers. They travel widely but tend to favor the "big mountains" for their home sites. There are even different races of Little People. They can be very friendly and helpful to humans. For example they may comfort frightened children or help a lost man out of the woods and set him on a course for home. If they feel so inclined the creatures may sneak in and do some chores for a family. The Little People can also cause mischief if the mood strikes them and if they feel it is deserved. Their shenanigans may range from harmless pranks to calculated torment that can drive one to madness. They have the power to do in a person as well.

An ancient story about the Little People had them enjoying fellowship and dance deep in the mountains one day. Their festivity was brought to an abrupt and solemn end when a herald came with news that Christ had died by crucifixion. The Yunwi Tsunsdi were so overcome with sadness that their teardrops turned to stone. The teardrops assumed the shape of tiny crosses.

Geologists tell us that the "fairy crosses" produced by the Little People are derived from crystals of a mineral called "staurolite." That name comes from the ancient Greek language and means "cross stone." Staurolite is a very common and wide-spread mineral, usually of muddy color. Colors vary by locality. The crystals have a prism-like shape and differ in size. Well developed crystals may show six distinct sides. The most sought-after staurolites are, indeed, the fairy crosses. They form into a cross shape, from two crystals, in what geologists call a "twinning" process. Sometimes a triple fusion of crystals provides a star shape. The single crystals are actually less common but not so widely collected.

Fairy crosses are said to bring good luck to people who possess them. There are regarded as a talisman or charm that will confer protection and a modicum of magic power. Some say they bring relief from depression and stress.

In Cherokee County, NC staurolite is spotted in only a few locations. Below Longtown, near the Andrews High School, is a site where the crystals are loosely scattered and tend to be poorly formed. Many well formed single (un-crossed) crystals have been collected from a small site in the Lunsford pasture. One has a better chance of finding the more common and highly sought after twin crosses on the old Dysart/Solomon property.

*****

"Longtown is haunted!" So many people will tell you. Many of the ghost stories about Longtown are centered in a particular area, up in Chambers Hollow and along the road between the old Chambers House (house D) and Tom Thomasson's old house (house T). That area may represent what some paranormal researchers call a "hot spot" of ghostly activity. A lady raised in the community said she always heard the road leading from Tom Thomasson's store was haunted. Another resident of Longtown would walk home from work at night with no fear until she reached that area, near the Thomasson/Bristol property line. "I was never afraid until I got there." she said. "Then I was scared to death that somebody would reach out and grab me before I got to [Tom Thomasson's] place."

A man who grew up in the community claimed to have heard, on multiple occasions, a sound akin to chains being dragged across the road as he walked home late at night. Once or twice he also heard the sound of a baby crying from a long- abandoned house a few yards past, and opposite, house F (the Matheson home).

Another story about this area of Longtown was repeatedly told by one of the Lunsford boys. He was walking home, late, on one very dark night. It was windy and a storm appeared to be brewing. He walked very quickly due to both fright and to the impending rain. All at once he noticed a well dressed woman, who held an unlit cigarette in her hand, walking next to him in the dark. She did not speak but moved the cigarette to her lips. As was good manners in those days, the boy was obliged to light the cigarette. He knew he had only one match and remembered thinking that it would never produce a fire in the fierce gusts of wind. The boy decided to go through the motions anyway. The match not only struck but held a flame as the wind whipped steadily by. The mysterious woman drew the flame into her cigarette. The boy looked down as he extinguished and dropped the match. In that instant the woman vanished. She was absolutely nowhere to be seen.

*****

A woman who had a lot of family members at Longtown told stories about the house in Chambers Hollow (house E). One of her grandmothers lived there and insisted the house was haunted. The other grandmother occupied the house at a different time in history and was as equally resolute that the house was nothing but normal. From this place, so the stories go, one could see bright lights in the woods on certain nights. Similar lights were supposedly visible across from house C. One of the Lunsford daughters said "children were afraid of that road."

Even in daylight, under the right conditions, that stretch of road could be unnerving. A man who grew up in the area recalled walking home from the theater in town after viewing the film *Ten Commandments* with its groundbreaking special effects and riveting Bible-based plot. The boy's companion ran ahead of him due to rumbling thunder and an impending storm. As the boy walked along he was terrified by a nervous horse in the Bristol pasture as well as by the brewing storm. Low-hanging, dark, billowy clouds added to the scene. That long, scary walk home has remained clear in the man's mind for decades.

*****

People who are inclined to believe in ghosts often say that some event in the distant past may be connected with paranormal activity. They reason that troubled spirits may be linked to those goings-on in the past in a cause-and-effect relationship. In other words, the hauntings form a cycle of tragedy through time.

Several people, especially older ones who had family living in the area for years, will tell you that a lynching took place during the Civil War era in the woods above Chambers Hollow. There are no details in their stories, just a statement of hearing about the event.

The Smoky Mountains, foothills and hollows of western North Carolina, eastern Tennessee and North Georgia were an essentially lawless place during the Civil War and even into the subsequent years which historians call "the reconstruction." Stories about "bushwhackers" and "renegades" from that era abound. The bushwhackers were active in a few remote areas, according to local tradition, even into the early to mid 1870s. Some were highly organized bands composed of either union or confederate soldiers. In other cases they were simply outlaws or deserters acting singly or in small groups. The common characteristic among bushwhackers was lawlessness. Their mission was to pillage and terrorize. Often the healthy men and boys of the households were gone away to battle. Aside from the efforts of the older men who comprised the Home Guard, that fact left the women and children very vulnerable. Food, valuables and clothing were often stolen. In many cases these items were not taken for use but were brazenly destroyed as citizens watched helplessly or fought futilely.

The old Valley Town settlement would have been a relatively short walk along the ridge and down a hollow or two from what would become Longtown. That community was a busy place during certain parts of the Civil War epoch. Allegedly there was a military camp along the present Aquone Street, near the old Leatherwood home. It is well acknowledged that people were killed, kidnapped and tortured in Valley Town. A hanging in the woods above Chambers Hollow seems very likely. Its documentation is as elusive as the ghost it may have produced. There is a well documented story of a woman living near the old Valley Town settlement who was tortured, by choking, with a rope. That may be the origin of the story about Chambers Hollow. Or...Supposedly, on certain nights, one can park their car in a particular place along the Old Mill Road to watch an eerie ball of light descend slowly down the hill.

*****

On the evening before Mr. Dysart was found dead, two of the Lunsford brothers claimed to have seen an apparition traveling through the fog-veiled woods at dusk near Chambers Hollow. One brother got a better look than the other did as he left to get the other's attention. The older brother claimed the specter looked like a well dressed soldier from the distant past riding along slowly on horseback.

*****

A handful of people still remember what surely must have been one of the most somber days at Longtown. In Chapter 6 of this book, poems titled *A Tribute to Mrs. G. W. Lunsford* and *Mother's Gone* concern the death of Conie Lunsford. Conie became seriously ill just days after the birth of her ninth child in March of 1928. In an almost unheard of journey to get better medical care, Mrs. Lunsford rode a train from Andrews to Asheville, NC where she died a few days later.

"Every neighbor and child was there when she left..." said one eyewitness. Conie Lunsford rode in a car to the railroad depot, about a mile away. People were in the Lunsford yard and on the large porch of the George Lunsford house to offer their assistance and moral support as the trip got underway. "I remember seeing Mrs. Lunsford raising her arm and waving goodbye to the ones that were on the porch at the time...She never came back."

*****

There are rare fragmentary accounts of a man being found frozen, dead from exposure, at a spring in Longtown. Some say the spring was located on the Long-Lunsford property. The spring mentioned in those stories was later enclosed and widely used in the community. Efforts to document this story have proven frustrating. There is likelihood that the death in question actually took place in another western North Carolina county and that the story was told by the surviving family members when they moved to Longtown. Such a story, involving a particular family from Longtown's distant past, is well documented in multiple sources. So it is possible that those who heard the account were confused and passed the tale to others, incorrectly, through time. Another variation of this story may stem from a woman being found dead nearer to, or upon parts of, the Bristol property. There was a hard freeze in the late 1930s to early 1940s and a woman died from exposure near a spring at her home.

*****

There is a thoroughly substantiated account of a tragic argument, chase and fight involving two members of a prominent Longtown family during the early years of the previous century. Newspapers as far away as Charlotte and Raleigh carried small stories about what they called "an affray" which resulted in the death of one of the parties. The two men were reported to have been engaged in an episode of drinking and gambling. Oral traditions declare that a card game was specifically at the root of the altercation. A lengthy argument and pursuit unfolded. The older man had a knife, the younger a gun. The actual killing took place in what would become the Lunsford pasture. While there were no witnesses, there was a finding that three bullets were fired into the older man and that he died instantly. He died with an open knife in his hand. The younger man claimed to have discharged the shots in self defense.

*****

Cora Thomasson always claimed to have seen an angel during the summer of 1932 when her niece Naomi died. Naomi Lunsford was Ora's daughter. She died at the age of 22 months on the front porch of Ora and George's house. Many people remembered hearing the child twice telling her parents that she was going to die.

*****

A man who lived most of his childhood in Longtown remembered being overcome by a sense of great tragedy and immense fear while walking alone in the forest near the Wells Spring when he was an adolescent. Even as a young boy he spent a great deal of time in the woods hiking and hunting. He was not one given to fear of the woods, nor to fear of isolation. His experience at that particular spot, on that particular day, left him with an eerie feeling which he never forgot. He said, "I remember running back home and asking Daddy if anything bad had ever happened up there. After that I usually made a quick trip in those woods or tried to avoid that part altogether." Even in recent times a woman reported periodically seeing an unusual, concentrated light rising up from a consistent spot in the Lunsford pasture.

*****

Two Longtown ghosts of a different type were Red Head and Bloody Bones. Their main job was to keep young children safe from accidents. That pair of spooks lived mostly in the upstairs rooms of the George Lunsford house. A granddaughter of Neil Lunsford reported that Bloody Bones also had digs in a back bedroom closet at her grandparents' house. He was also known to frequently hang around a set of steps which led to the main road below the house.

*****

For a time, Longtown had its own "peeping tom." The young man spent the daylight hours asleep in his family's barn loft. At night he would rove around the community, either on foot or while riding a donkey, to spy on his neighbors. This man would look through windows to see what people were having for supper or to see what they were doing for entertainment. Nearly everyone in the neighborhood regarded him as annoying, but harmless, and felt no real sense of threat from him. He did get chased away by frustrated Longtown citizens on more than one occasion.

*****

Most everyone knows a story about the man who moved to North Carolina as a young boy and eventually brought global attention to Andrews when he became the subject of a nation-wide manhunt. How many remember the manhunt for Mr. Clarence Chambers decades earlier? An intense search was launched for him but for entirely different reasons. When the Associated Press picked up the story, they did not mention the Longtown Community by name but did note that Mr. Chambers had been visiting at Andrews when he was bitten on the finger by the family dog. In an effort to be proactive and save Clarence's life, a massive search was launched when it was discovered that the pet had rabies. Image 5-25 shows a newspaper clipping from 1954.

Search Ends, Life Saved

AFTER a nation-wide search for Clarence Chambers, 34, the construction worker receives the first of 21 anti-rabies injections from a nurse at Fresno County Hospital. Chambers, working at Redding, was found on a bus by state highway patrolmen Friday and was notified that his dog, which bit him on a finger a week ago at his home in Andrews, N. C., died of the disease.—(AP Wirephoto.)

Image 5-25: A 1954 newspaper clipping detailing a happy ending for Longtown native son Clarence Chambers.

*****

Emma White Hogan was raised in the Junaluska community of Cherokee County. As a young girl, she made regular trips to the areas surrounding Longtown for extended visits with friends and relatives. One such trip, from around the mid 1930s, stood out in her mind. It was then that she saw an air show featuring Joe Musleh.

Mr. Joseph Henry Musleh was a skilled pilot who made the bulk of his living with an airplane throughout much of the southeastern United States. He would sometimes take paying passengers on sightseeing flights. However, Musleh was mostly known for his flashier, dangerous stunt flying. Some called him a "barnstormer" referencing low-flying, noisy jaunts to keep his public excited. Sometimes other pilots would join him on the air shows. The site of flying planes was novel enough to folks in this area. Parachutists would sometimes add to the crowd-thrilling display. The show Emma Hogan witnessed as a 10 year old girl was a major attraction in Andrews that day. Ms. Hogan recalled walking a trail through the woods to Leatherwood Mountain with Lou Patterson and sisters 'Nita Rogers and Pawnee Rogers Wooten (along with others) to get a good view.

Joe Musleh and his flying stunts were widely written about in newspapers from the 1930s. An article from Burlington, North Carolina's *Daily Times* in January of 1938 noted Musleh as "one of the South's outstanding pilots…[who has] flown for 13 years without a single accident to mar his record." Sadly, the same paper reported that on October 20, 1938, thirty-five year old Musleh "…was killed instantly when his tri-motored passenger plane crashed near here today." Emma Hogan was privileged to see a historic show featuring the legendary Joe Musleh in his prime only about two years before his tragic death.

*****

Most of the families who lived at Longtown made do with very little in the way of material possessions during early days. As Gene Palmer recalled, most of the houses had no running water inside. The Palmer house had an outside sink from which water drained into a nearby field. Gene's dad, Billy Palmer, primarily made his living as a blacksmith and a machinist in iron mines. Sometimes the two, along with Billy's son Bud, found short stints of work in the tannery at Andrews. During the Great Depression times were extremely hard in terms of being able to find paying work. The

Palmers shared what little they had and likely saved some of their neighbors from starvation on more than one occasion.

*****

Gasoline was cheap in the 1930s and early 1940s but money was hard to come by, especially for young boys who wanted to joy ride. Wade and Jack Lunsford's father, George, worked at the tannery in Andrews and knew the ins and outs of the tanning process better than just about anyone in town. In later times, he practically ran the place by himself after years of working his way up the ranks.

One step of the hide tanning procedure involved soaking the skins in gasoline. The tannery had large cisterns of gas just for that purpose. It was used over and over and was rarely changed. In time, the gasoline in those tannery tanks would become very thick and turn almost black.

George Lunsford gave, likely against his better judgment, permission for his teenage boys to collect some of the oldest, sludgiest tannery gas for use as automobile fuel. Jack and Wade didn't mind the murky, thick, black cloud of smoke that followed them around (and loomed behind them) as they motored along. They were just thrilled to have a free source of "pant'er piss" when they wanted to ride and could get a car. The police, on the other hand, did not think it was such a good idea. The boys were forced to abandon their plan to recycle gas from the tannery vats as the streets of town filled with a lingering black fog.

*****

A few people who were tiny children in the 1940s still remember "the wreck." Longtown was host to a number of auto accidents over the course of time and this must have been one of the earliest. Nobody was hurt but people poured out of their houses to watch the aftermath. Some stood on porches; others went down to speak to the parties involved.

A group of youngsters snuck out to the site of the accident with great curiosity. They kept trying to catch a good look at the legs of one of the car drivers. The children whispered among themselves as they carefully studied the man's feet from a safe distance. They pointed, whispered some more and hoped that the man's pants legs would ride up to give them a better view.

Why were the children so interested in the man's legs; so focused on his feet? Well…in the first moments after the accident they heard an adult say "He's just an old bootlegger!"

*****

People who were sitting on George Lunsford's front porch on a certain summer evening in the 1970s can still laugh out loud when they think of a complicated series of events that nobody except George Lunsford could have linked together. Mr. Lunsford had a rarely used, mischievous sense of humor. His advanced age (90 plus) and mild hearing loss may also have figured into the events as they unfolded.

There was a middle aged couple who lived in one of the rental houses at the time of this story. People liked them and they were both very nice to children. Most of the time, the couple could be described as being good neighbors. They were friendly but kept to themselves. Mostly they were a very quiet, reserved couple. However, the duo had a sad and serious weakness for alcohol. About once each month they would drink themselves into a fix. Then came the argument. The intoxicated husband and wife would engage in what could only be described as a loud, old fashioned "cuss fight" until the effects of the alcohol faded. The altercations almost never became physical but would grow louder and louder and louder until one of them passed out. The language involved could embarrass a drunken sailor.

On this same day, George Lunsford's son Wade was in the middle of an extended visit from his home at Maryland. Wade liked to do special things for his parents when he visited. On this trip, Wade brought some sound recordings of church services. He thought that George and Ora may enjoy hearing the old fashioned singing and preaching on the tapes. So, during the evening Wade hooked up a bulky eight track tape player and speakers on the porch with the aid of electrical extension cords.

The neighbors' cuss fight was just beginning to brew at about the time the George Lunsford family assembled on the porch. The argument was still at a normal conversational tone and only occasionally breached the banter on the Lunsford porch. Everyone at the Lunsford house that evening settled in for visiting and conversation. Slowly the neighbors' argument escalated in both severity and in volume. The bickering, heavily laced with expletives, was soon in full swing. Children were present on the Lunsford porch so an uncomfortable aura quickly developed. The language from the rental house grew more and more sharp, more and more vulgar and more and more difficult to ignore. All the bad words were in play; nothing was held back from either the man or the woman. Something had to be done.

With no explanation Wade Lunsford stuck a tape into the player. He tried to adjust the volume for his dad to comfortably hear the recording of the church services and loud enough to drown out the cuss fight that was growing ever more thunderous.

Within a short time span, George Lunsford began to inexplicably snigger every few moments. Then he began to giggle and chuckle more obviously. It took his family a few minutes to catch on. George would listen keenly, and then laugh more and more. His face turned red with amusement. Laughter literally brought tears to the eyes of those on the porch as George finally said, "I want you to listen to that bunch over there. Have you ever heard anything to beat that in your life? They'll cuss a while and then they'll sing a hymn." George laughed so hard he could hardly breathe. He did manage to add, between giggles, "When that preacher leaves, we'll sneak over there and get us a drink."

*****

The George Lunsford house at Longtown is well remembered as a gathering place for people of all ages. George had a large family and many of his children's friends regularly came for a visit, an overnight stay and/or a meal. As one friend of Lunsford daughter Wilma said, "The doors were always open. There was always room for one more in the family." George's son Cecil had a stream of friends who visited him at Longtown on a regular basis. One of many good stories from Cecil's gang of friends involved Dennis Raxter, who grew up in the nearby Happytop Community, and Gene Webb (a friend from town).

Gene knew a lot about cars. He and his brother Sam taught many people to drive over the years. One day the three boys (Gene, Dennis and Cecil) were traveling down the road in Gene's truck. Only Gene knew that he had been doing some work on the truck just a few hours prior to the pleasure trip. He had taken off the steering wheel during his work. Gene had positioned the wheel back in place on the steering column but had not yet bolted it down. As the boys sped down the road, Dennis began to complain about Gene's driving. He was stunned and flabbergasted when

Gene lifted off the steering wheel, handed it to him and said, "Well here, you drive awhile then!"

*****

The following incredible story could have come directly from the pen of a Hollywood script writer. In the 1950s a young boy who lived at Longtown was walking home from a lengthy day of school. He took a shortcut across the yard of a long-abandoned house site on what many people today call the "practice field" at the present-day Andrews High School property. The little boy was mostly interested in unwinding, having supper and playing once he reached home. As he was chattering away to his mother that evening the boy happened to mention that he had heard unusual sounds (which reminded him of a person struggling in water) while he followed his route homeward. The woman's immediate reaction was to ask her son to retrace his journey while she followed. The mother's quick thinking, along with the boy's casual summary of the day's events, saved a life. The pair found a man nearly dead from exhaustion, struggling to stay buoyant in an old well. It seems the man had been walking by innocently enough when old boards intended to seal the well gave way. Help was quickly dispatched. The man was rescued and the well was filled with rocks and dirt.

*****

Dick and Emma Hogan had one of the first televisions in the community. That, coupled with their natural hospitality and good nature, made the Hogan household a favorite gathering place for many neighborhood children. The Hyde children, in particular, enjoyed coming to the house for popcorn, TV and social time with Hogan sons Bobby and Russell. The western-themed series *Wagon Train* was a special favorite. Adults admired the yard filled with an unrivaled assortment of trees, flowers and other landscaping pleasures. The yard, in fact, remains interesting and beautiful all year long. Almost anyone who has been associated with Longtown since the late 1950s makes a point to mention the Hogan family as being the absolute best of neighbors.

*****

Doris, Gene, Irma, Jack, Lucy and Pat were a group of Longtown neighbors and chums who would often walk to school together in the

1930s and 1940s. They, and sometimes other friends, would file out of their individual houses in the mornings and join one another along the way. Before they reached school, they were all together and enjoyed the rest of the walk in one large group. One spring morning the group spied a bed of the most beautiful yellow tulips they had ever seen growing inside a garden fence near the Herbert house. Exactly how many separate days Gene sneaked over the fence to retrieve a tulip for Lucy is not known. What is known is that Mrs. Herbert kept missing her tulips until, one day; she did some investigative work and put an end to the escapades.

*****

In the 1930s T. J. Thomasson Jr. was one of the few students in Andrews who not only had access to a car, but who was also sometimes allowed to drive it to school. In those days, children got a one hour lunch break. Some of them stayed at school and ate a lunch they brought with them. Many others would go home to eat. Some were lucky enough to get a fully cooked meal. T. J.'s car must have been a funny sight as he came home for lunch. The seats were filled to overflowing with friends, and practically all the neighbor children from Longtown, who caught a ride. In fact, the running boards on the car were loaded with passengers as well. T. J. drove slowly enough that children simply stepped off the car as he passed by their respective houses. An hour later…you guessed it…The car would fill up again as "Junior Thomasson" headed the car back to School House Hill with his neighbors and friends hanging on and standing on the running boards.

Tom Thomasson

The White Cabin

Our little white cabin has never been amiss
It's occupied at present by kindhearted "Ode and Sis"
No better neighbors can be found, in fact they don't exist.
They live among the native pines, kindhearted Ode and Sis

They are very optimistic, good deeds they don't resist
They are always very jovial, kindhearted Ode and Sis
They have two fine children they love, caress and kiss
They are the joy and pride of kindhearted Ode and Sis

I know that they will teach them to shun the evil list
And obey their loving parents, kindhearted Ode and Sis
May they find, when life is o'er a perfect home of bliss
For their hardships here below, kindhearted Ode and Sis

Dear Stella Mae

January 12, 1941

I got your letter by the way.
I am trying now to repay
It was the best I've ever had
and tickled me, I say real bad
I would have answered you before,
but have been doing more and more
To build more cabins in my town.
You cannot keep a good man down
The last one now among the pines,
above "Tom Cotter's" all in line
The finest yet looks like a treat,
with lights and water all complete
It sits away up on the bank.
I pulled a useful little prank
By moving Wilson's old woodshed.
There's room enough for just one bed

There's three small rooms, but very nice.
Just room enough for man and wife
I'm sure the tenants like it well.
If they pay me for it, I will tell
Tell Zeke the "britches" fit me well.
If not she is not here to tell
Tell her I thank her more and more,
because my other pants I tore
Tell Bert I got my corn today.
It came in handy too; I say
The hens were despondent by the way.
They wouldn't even try to lay
Now write me soon, do not delay.
A visit soon you all must pay
A disappointment is too bad
for Jane and Jackie's great granddad

Pearly's Summer Home

Pearly chose an abrupt spot
Above our town, an abrupt lot
Upon that lot his mind was fixed
To build a home among the sticks

With survey curving through those sticks
A driveway then was quickly fixed
With traffic trouble all passed by
To drive the scenic curve in high

One mile from town, a mammoth fill
Directs you 'round the scenic hill
Up to a mound of native pines
To where the scenic driveway winds.

Here on the lawn, beneath the trees
We praise the Lord for Nature's breeze
And wonder why there are so few
Who build their homes 'round scenic views

This home when fully made complete
Will be a model place to sleep
The breeze through the native pines
Will cheer your heart and soothe your mind

We often hear the whippoorwill
Your mind, it seems, it wants to thrill
And then we hear around the trails
The cheering chirps of the nightingales

A health resort for everyone
Who wants pure air and radiant sun
With fragrance sweet and cooling shades
That God for all of us has made

The scenery 'round this place is grand
With mountain peaks and rolling lands
Should cause more folks to come and see
Where many summer homes should be

We see great wonders 'round the balds
Above the peaks our eagle squalls
Down 'neath the cliffs and evergreens
The vicious panther sometimes screams

There's babbling brooks and bubbling springs
There's speckle trout and birds to sing
There's flowers for the honey bees
There's chattering squirrels up in the trees

The hemlock, spruce and native pine
Sing through the breeze a welcomed chime
Come on ye people brave and free
Five thousand feet above the sea

Chapter 6

Longtown and "The Town," Part Two

COMMENTARY: Chapter Introduction

Tom Thomasson lived at Longtown and within "his town" for nearly fifty years. Some of his children lived there even longer. Tom's daughter Cora was there well into the 1990s. So, a second chapter is crucial to a documentation of the history. In this continuation from Chapter 5 the lives of Tom Thomasson, his neighbors, tenants and family are chronicled in poetry and song over an approximately thirty year period. Editorial comments and clarifications are offered as deemed useful.

Many of the poems in this chapter are tributes to neighbors and family friends. Tom seemed to have a special gift for poetizing young children and adolescents. This skill is evidenced in selections like *Judy McClain*, *Juanita* and *Caroline*. Another item, *Mary's Birthday: February 22, 1934*, captures the mood of a gathering to celebrate George Lunsford's daughter and her "coming of age." There are even poems paying tribute to faithful pets Sport and Spot. Sprinkled throughout the writings comprising this set are lessons on morality.

The final entry for this chapter is a song called *Longtown Blues*. Readers may think of *Longtown Blues* as a sort of "answer song" to Tom's *Peachtree Blues*, presented at the close of Chapter 2. Although Tom Thomasson made frequent short trips back to his previous community of Peachtree, he never made a permanent move. Tom seemed mostly very content at Longtown but lyrics from the refrain to *Longtown Blues* ("I am leaving Longtown soon. I can't stand these weary blues") suggest a move crossed his mind.

In Memory of Mrs. Wilson

Mother's gone our precious darling
She left us lonely here today
She's now with God and her loved ones
The Angels bore her soul away

It was sad to give up mother
Almost more than we could bear
But we submitted all to him
Who helps us – our burdens bear

She was kind to everybody
Full of truth and love and grace
But God saw fit to take her
To a happier, better place.

She's now with little David
And many loved ones up there
Above the stars in glory
Up in heaven – somewhere

A noble heart this mother had
Though she was very plain
To labor she would do her part
But seldom did complain

She was a model mother
With Carlee by her side
To assist in all her efforts
And help to her provide

I'm sure that over Jordan
Beyond the rolling tide
She'll receive a great reward
And with the good abide

May her circle be unbroken
As her toilsome life is o'er
And may we all be gathered
On that happy golden shore

We'll hold to God's unchanging hand
'Till eternal life we gain
Up there we'll hear the Angels say
"Shake hands with Mother again"

Note: The subject of this poem is Mary Collins Wilson who died in 1937. She was married to W. O. Wilson who passed away in 1946. Carlee Wilson Best was Mrs. Wilson's daughter. Two of her children, Dave and Mary Frances died in childhood. The family recalled that David was very ill and that one of the Bristol men in the neighborhood drove him to the hospital at Sylva.

Juanita

Juanita is a model girl. No better can be found
She doesn't even want to flirt and never loafers town
She dresses very common. She doesn't like a flirt
She shuns their very presence. From them she always shirks
Her sisters are good scholars; they help this girl to teach
To be so sweet and lovely and keep so nice and neat

She wears a suit of pretty hair, as black as any crow
She finds a host of lovers wherever she may go
Her cheeks are like two cherries. Her eyes are sparkling bright
They sparkle when she's smiling, just like the stars at night
She does most all the errands about the place you see
They couldn't do without her, it doesn't look to me

I think she is a model, as nice as she can be
She helps to do the washing and helps to fix the tea
She washes all the dishes, for no one else she waits
She fixes up the parlor and there her lessons take
She sweeps off all the porches, then hurries off to school
She studies well her subjects, observing every rule

There's no better than Juanita, to homefolks she is dear
Her little friends admire her, because she's full of cheer.
I know she is a model for all the girls around
She always helps her mamma and never loafers town
She always loves her Papa. She loves her mama dear
Her brothers and her sisters. And Uncle Tom out there

Old Sport

J. H:

Your favorite dog "Old Sport" is dead
The one you most admired -- you said
You turned her over to my care
But then her care I soon did share

I hated much to see Sport go
Because she seemed to love me so
Indeed she had much great respect
Much love for me, that is correct

One day a snake bit her right hand,
She said its more than I can stand
Oh! Sir, it seemed she tried to say
It hurts me awful bad today

I bathed her hand and rubbed it well
Prepared a shade up by the well
She thanked me much and tried to tell
With many pranks and many yells

Old Sport and I became great friends
Each one the other's pranks did lend
Until one day we had to part,
It seemed like it would break my heart

A roaring school bus came dashing by
Where me and Sport was standing nigh
Into the wheels a dash she gave,
I'm sure my life she meant to save

She was a dog with conscience clean
The nicest dog I've ever seen,
If there's a place where good dogs go
She's got a place up there I know

A Tribute to Mrs. G. W. Lunsford

March 30, 1928

Oh, we are sad and lonesome since death came the other day
And took Mrs. Conie Lunsford from our midst, alas to stay
She leaves a model husband and nine children here to mourn
We pray that God will help them to meet her 'round the throne

We miss her, yes we miss her, we miss her one and all
For like our loving mother she helped at every call.
She was always kind and cheerful, and met us with a smile
She had a word of comfort, for every little child

And we, too, all her neighbors, who around her bedside stayed
Will surely all remember when the debt of death she paid.
And how she braved death's battle and counseled one and all
To meet her high in glory when God sends forth his call

Now we, with all her loved ones, must to God's will submit
And her words of cheer and comfort, we'll surely not forget
So when this life is ended and the dead in Christ shall rise
May we meet Mrs. Conie Lunsford above the starry skies

Note: Mrs. G. W. Lunsford died March 27, 1928 at an Asheville hospital. G. W. and Conie were Tom Thomasson's neighbors. Following Conie's death, Tom Thomasson's daughter, Ora, married Mr. Lunsford. An alternative copy of the poem ends with the line "We want to meet Mrs. Lunsford above the star-lit skies." A clarification about Mrs. Lunsford's name is of note. Her middle name was "Gecona." She often spelled her nickname as "Cona" or "Conie." In at least one case she spelled it "Coney."

Mother's Gone

For Annie Lunsford

Mother's gone our darling mother
We don't know why she went away
And left our broken hearted daddy
And nine children here to pray

God had some hidden motive
For He doeth all things well
We'll try to be submissive
And let the future tell

Our home's so sad without her
Who lies upon the hill
To rest in peaceful slumber
Oh! why was it God's will?

Our home is sad and lonely
Since mother went away
She said that she would meet us
On some blessed happy day

Yes she's gone our darling mother
But her place I'll try to fill
I'll teach my baby brother
And council darling Dill

I'll lay away my school books
I'll lay aside my play
I'll take up mother's duties
I'll work and I will pray

We all must stay together
Daddy said we surely could
The girls around will help us
They said they always would

I'm willing to contribute
All my time and talent too
To home and little loved ones
'til my life on Earth is through

And when this life is over
Which like an arrow flies
I want to meet my mother
Beyond the sparkling skies

Note: Tom Thomasson had this tribute published in a local paper but credited the authorship to Annie Lunsford, daughter of Conie Lunsford. In the piece, "Dill" refers to her brother Dillie.

Our Definition of the Kenneth Jones Family as Good Neighbors

The Joneses are our neighbors, we've got along quiet well
With very little friction, as everyone can tell.
They are our good Samaritans. They don't refrain at all
To come to our assistance and help at every call

They are a model couple, with model children three
They surely are as happy as any folks could be.
We know they're strictly honest, on them we can depend
To meet their obligations, every effort they will bend

They are always on the alert, as busy as the bees,
But we like to hear them clatter, especially that feisty cute Louise
They are very optimistic and seldom take the blues,
But look across the waters to find the best to choose

They are always kind and jovial and sober every day
In every conversation, have something kind to say.
They are very sympathetic and always do their best
To provide for every one they find in deep distress

Their little words of kindness and splendid deeds of love
Has gained for them much glory, that will shine for them above
We like to see them prosper, in this old world so wide
And like to help to prize them, above the rolling tide

The height of their ambition, as we have each one seen
Is teach their children kindness, with manners in between
Sometimes we get contrary, and then we don't agree
But when we talk things over, we're happy as can be

We know we're only human, and each one have our faults
But when our conscience lashes, we quickly turn across
We have done our best to flatter and keep them with us here
We'll still try to high-tone them, for at least another year

When we can't keep them longer, we'll hate it mighty bad
Because they are the best neighbors, I guess we've ever had
When they can stay no longer, and we are far apart
We hope we'll still be neighbors at least down in our hearts

COMMENTARY: Mr. Jefferson Davis Dysart

One of The Town's most storied residents, Jeff Dysart, was the subject of the following poem. The poem appears to be as much about his caregivers as it is about Mr. Dysart. Mattie Matheson was a long-time community resident. Ora, of course, was Tom Thomasson's daughter. Dollie Mae Lunsford was the first wife of Ray Lunsford, George Lunsford's son. They, along with many others who lived nearby, kept a constant check on the welfare of Jeff Dysart as he aged and grew sicker.

Tom Thomasson selected words and phrases like pest, pessimistic and "a scene of pity" to describe Dysart. Others who knew him may have at least partially disagreed. It may be that an adjective such as "misunderstood" could have been more appropriate. Mr. Dysart originally lived near The Town, behind the George Lunsford property, on land that would later come to be known as the "Solomon Place." In his later years Mr. Dysart lived in the small house (house E) in the hollow behind the Matheson homestead.

Surprisingly few details about Dysart's personal life persist. His gravesite communicates an air of great sadness and gloom. Someone with a good heart and respect for the dead took the trouble to place a small, well marked stone tile. On the right-hand side it is inscribed "Wife of Jeff Dysart." Mr. Dysart's name (J. D. Dysart) is on the left. There are neither dates nor verses. That stone is, perhaps, symbolic of Mr. Dysart's life. There is little to say.

Mr. Dysart was born in 1861 in a town named for his family, Dysartsville NC. That town is situated in McDowell County. His wife's name was Margaret. She was born either in Indiana or Virginia and was often called "Maggie." Dysart mostly made his living with the railroad. For a time he lived in Nebraska. Indications are that Dysart married late in life. Apparently there were no children. The earliest definitive record of his living in Andrews NC is from 1918. The 1920 census taker noted that Jeff Dysart made his living as a farmer.

People who knew Jeff Dysart reasonably well recalled that he was retired from the railroad and, originally, fairly well off financially. His earliest home site near Andrews could best be described as a country estate. It was originally accessible by way of a country dirt road at Longtown, beginning within the Lunsford property (see Image 5-1, Chapter 5). In more recent times the property was accessible along Colvard Avenue. Between about 1918 and about 1924 Mr. Dysart amassed nearly 70 acres of real estate. There was a large house with beautiful grounds of pastures and woods. There were outbuildings and shops. There was an apple orchard and stately specimen trees. A small pond held a pet fish, named Drum, which had been conditioned to respond to Dysart's hand gestures. Inside the house were all sorts of fine furnishings, including antiques. Mr. Dysart also had a respectable collection of rocks and minerals.

Exactly what turned the tide on Jeff Dysart's lifestyle is not known. He died blind, and practically a pauper, in the early1940s. Some legal trouble regarding a property line came to a head in 1920. That matter appeared to resolve. Dysart purchased additional property adjoining his holdings. An action of foreclosure followed in January of 1924. Mrs. Dysart died in 1927 following a struggle with heart inflammation. Before too much longer Jeff Dysart was at the absolute mercy of neighbors and friends. He knew a few people in the town of Andrews, notably Mr. Sandlin. Those two may have befriended one another through their work on the railroad. Otherwise it appears that a group of Dysart's neighbors made a pact to see that he had a place to live and food to eat. One is left to speculate whether Mr. Dysart may have lost his pension due to the national economic climate of the day.

As he began to grow older, and after his wife died, Dysart's health began to fail miserably. His eyesight, in particular, was very bad. He lived alone. More than a handful of people, kids and adults, would habitually sneak around Mr. Dysart's houses. They usually came in the late evening and at night to scare him, to play tricks on him, or to steal from him. So Dysart developed a very cautious outlook on people and a superficially rough, bad-tempered persona. If he knew you well, so the accounts go, he was good to you. He would talk to you and tell interesting stories. He would loan out his tools, all of which he had carefully initialed "J. D." with a sharp awl. He was grateful for meals which were regularly carried to him, mostly by the Lunsford boys, later in his life. A daughter of George Lunsford recalled that Mr. Dysart had affection for her family. Ora Thomasson Lunsford sent Mr. Dysart more than a full meal at least daily. George would help with odd chores around Dysart's house.

A funny story about Mr. Dysart occurred when he lived at the Solomon place. It seems that he had put in a hard "wash day" as so many people in that era did at least once a week. Dysart drained his wash pot and propped up his "punching stick" nearby. A punching stick, by the way, was used to stir clothes and dip them from the hot water. There was one piece of laundry that Jeff Dysart neglected to process. It may have been a rag used to dry his hands. Since he was tired he threw the cloth over the punching stick to dry. That night there was a very bright moon. Some out-of-the-ordinary sound caught Mr. Dysart's attention and he walked out of doors to investigate. At some point he retrieved his ancient shotgun, with its square barrel, from inside the house. Mr. Dysart's failing eyesight, his paranoia and his record of bad experiences with bad people brought the events to a climax. He demanded to know who was lurking about in his yard so late at night. He could see a vague outline, the shape of a head perhaps, yards in front of him and in the farthest reaches of his vision. The figure remained mysteriously and forebodingly silent as he slowly approached it. Bad vision and paranoia made Dysart question whether the figure was actually moving toward him. He yelled repeated warnings into the darkness. Mr. Dysart's calls continued to go unanswered. He warned again and then pulled the trigger. Mr. Dysart blew his wash pot to hell.

Some of the Lunsford boys found Mr. Dysart dead one November evening as they took supper to him. Their father, George, attended to Mr. Dysart's body and had the authorities in town notified. It was reported that some very corrupt things went on to "settle the estate" of Mr. Dysart. The few known details will not be recounted.

Tom Thomasson

Gone - - But not Forgotten

For Mrs. Mattie Matheson, Ora and Dollie Mae

Mr. Dysart was a being
Who stayed right by himself
Very few would go about him
Because he was a "pest"

Some old girls in our village
No difference who they are
Decided with each other
To look for his welfare

He was a scene of pity
No one with him akin
Those girls did assist him
They were good Samaritans

He was very pessimistic
And wicked by the way
But he being human
They fed him every day

They asked him many questions
About his soul's welfare
With little consolation
But of course they did not despair

They quoted him some scripture
Then sang for him a song
He groaned and then he murmured
"That was a pretty song."

They must have all been praying
While to him each day they trod
That Jesus Christ would save his soul
And take it home to God

They should all be very thankful
That they felt duty bound
To go to his assistance
Before he did go down

No doubt they all feel happy
They've brightened up their crowns
All set with extra diamonds
That will forever shine

Mary's Birthday: February 22, 1934

'twas on the twenty-second
Where as above is seen
We ate with Mary Lunsford
When she was sweet sixteen

'twas fine indeed to watch her
When she would forward lean
With a real welcome to her guests
When she was sweet sixteen

She and Ruby faced each other
Hazel and I between
The other girls ate at our side
When she was sweet sixteen

It was a splendid dinner
No better has been seen
But it was quickly over
When she was sweet sixteen

This was a happy party
I think there were thirteen
We all was very jolly
When she was sweet sixteen

When we had heartily eaten
We felt a wee bit mean
Without a single present
When she was sweet sixteen

We won't forget the party
She won't forget the scene
When she came in we kissed her
When she was sweet sixteen

She wore a smile of beauty
As pretty as a queen
At that nice birthday dinner
When she was sweet sixteen

Her hair was brown and wavy
She wore a suit of green
She was so kind and cheerful
When she was sweet sixteen

Now this was universal
As though she were a queen
The nation celebrated
When she was sweet sixteen

It was a fine occasion
The best we've ever seen
But we'll never have another
When she is *just* sixteen

Judy McClain

Judy is our little friend. She lives with her grandma
Who teachers her with patience to no one else annoy
She teaches her the gospel and many other things
She taught her good manners. She taught her how to sing

She sings so nice and sweetly. It makes our village ring
That is much more important than doing worthless things
She plays with other children and sings with them so nice
They surely do admire her and treat her very nice

She has had one year in school and passed in all her grades
She studies well all her books and never cross marks made
Miss Jones her lovely teacher to her was very kind
Because she was submissive, her teacher she did mind

She likes to help her grandma but she likes to play at school
She teaches all her playmates to never break the rules
Such little girls are welcome at their home or abroad
For they are very useful to our own blessed Lord

Old Spot

Written for Betty Thomasson, June 20, 1955

Old Spot is one of my best friends.
My business he tries to attend
He seems my where-a-bouts to know
and walks with me where e'er I go.
He stands and wags his bushy tail.
He watches every road and trail
When things go wrong he always yells,
for that's the way he has to tell

When I lie down at night to sleep,
I know he will my welfare keep
When Old Spot barks the cowards run,
but if he growls I get my gun
Most everyone admires Old Spot,
because he's always on the dot
He recognizes every one.
It doesn't differ when they come

Old Spot's instinct is very great,
perhaps the finest in the state
A genius of the whole dog tribe,
his name is now known far and wide
Old Spot is worth his weight in gold,
no matter where he is or where he goes
To anyone who wants to buy,
the price on Spot is not too high

Tom Thomasson

Caroline

For David and Louise

We have a little sister
Her name is Caroline
We think that she's the sweetest girl
That we have ever seen

Her hair is black as ravens
Her eyes are both deep blue
We know that when you see her
You'll say that she's sweet too

Mamma cut her hair today
It made us each one mad
But saw it was so pretty
We both were very glad

We love our little sister
She's just began to coo
And when we are kind to her
We know she loves us too

Sometimes she cries a little
Just about every night
There's nothing hurts her badly
I guess she wants a light

For when the light is "litten"
She opens up her eyes
As playful as a kitten
No more our baby cries

It won't be long till baby
Will go with us to school
We think that baby sister
Will never break a rule

When we to school are going
We'll skip and romp and play
And when the school is over
We'll hurry home each day

We'll tell the truth to mamma
We'll tell the truth to dad
Because we know that is better
And know we'd better had

COMMENTARY: Business and Community Endeavors

Despite the fact that Longtown was an informal borough there were threads of community organization from its earliest days. The territory was by no means self contained. However, there were some surprising facets to the community of which most people are unaware today. It would have been possible to live at Longtown in isolation, but not completely practical. This section will explore some of the businesses, work and community endeavors which could have been found in the early days.

Almost everyone had a small garden. Some had large fields (see Image 6-1). Many families kept cattle, chickens and other animals. Water was abundant. Before it was piped to the houses, clean water was available with expenditure of some effort. A short walk to a spring, with a bucket in hand, was required. Two or three of the houses had a well. Citizens of "The Town" all had their own skills. Some were good at sharpening tools; others could mend shoes, sew clothing or make quilts. Just about everyone knew how to preserve meat and vegetables of various kinds by drying, canning or pickling. Men and women alike could shoot well enough to bring in game like squirrels or rabbits and the occasional bear or deer. Hogs were usually slaughtered around Thanksgiving each year (see Image 6-2). Abundant woodland provided fuel for cook stoves and fireplaces. Many people had a spring box for cooling perishables.

Image 6-1: George Lunsford cutting his garden with a disc in the 1940s. Mandy, ever gentle with children, was his helper. Behind Mandy's back is the top of house Q. Behind Mr. Lunsford is the hillside where house R sat.

In later years a few people called on Mr. Webb, who lived below the town of Andrews, to deliver ice right to their doors. You could also order custom delivered milk. A half-pint glass bottle of chocolate milk was a welcome special treat for the children at Neil Lunsford's house. "They had the best chocolate milk!" someone else recalled, speaking of Hall's Dairy at Murphy. "I also can remember the driver who delivered milk telling about the chocolate cow!"

Image 6-2: A hog killing such as the one pictured above was an annual tradition at the George Lunsford house. Lunsford is pictured with neighbors who remain unidentified.

Times were safe enough for small children to pull a wagon containing corn a couple of miles and then return from the Old Mill Road with cornmeal. Many of the men, and some of the women, had jobs in town. Big specialized stores were less than a mile's walk away. The children mostly attended centralized town schools. Longtown had a few things to draw in people from town and beyond. There were houses to rent. Some people came to buy food and other items.

*****

The "slaughter pen" was mentioned briefly in Chapter Five. The pen was basically a fenced-enclosed area which included a slaughter house. It was there where livestock, mostly cows, raised for food was killed. The site was an origin for names of other landmarks in the community as well (e.g. Slaughter Pen Curve). Not too much history about the slaughter pen and slaughter house is known. Tom Thomasson mentions the slaughter pen in the poem *Just a Stroll: 1934* which was presented in Chapter Five. A resident of the community who remembered the operation being active in her childhood thought that the Bristols may have owned the land at some point in time. Another with recollections about the establishment was Lil Long Love. She remembered that most of the meat which was processed at the slaughter house was ultimately sent to one of the grocery stores in town. The approximate location of the complex is shown on Image 5-1.

Emma White Hogan recalled that to a group of small children, the slaughter house was a dark and creepy place. She and other youngsters used to scare one another while walking through the structure on a dare. A man who grew up in Longtown told stories about the small stream running out of Dysart Hollow routinely turning red with blood during especially heavy work days. A lady recalling "peeping in" the slaughter house when she was a child used words like "bloody" and "nasty" to describe the scene. A funny story about the slaughter pen had Emma White seeing a fox for the first time in her life. The creature was sitting on a hillside, within the pen, chewing on an old cow's head. Long after the slaughter pen and slaughter house ceased operation, neighborhood children playing at the site would sometimes find old bones washed out after a rain.

*****

Mention of the numerous country stores Tom Thomasson operated in his life has been repeatedly made in this book. He had one at Longtown as well. In those days, country stores were the norm in rural communities. Some were housed in stand-alone buildings (such as one Tom had at Peachtree) and other stores were operated out of front rooms or side rooms in peoples' homes. Country stores of the era were somewhat akin to the convenience stores of today. Similar businesses (at least three of them) were in operation in the nearby Happy Top community as well. The Best family, former Longtown residents, operated one there well into the 1970s. Despite the fact that "The Town" was less than one mile away from the business district of Andrews, NC, Tom Thomasson did a steady trade at his country store. "We shopped at his store quite often." one person reported.

Many people in the earlier years did not have cars. For others taxis were a luxury. Some households had a car. But it was often in use by the family breadwinner, and not usually available for shopping trips, until weekends. A lot of people made the walk to town multiple times through the week. However, the chore of lugging home groceries by hand made the nearby Thomasson's Cash Store an appealing alternative.

"When you said 'going to the store' that's what you meant, striking out to Mr. Thomasson's store. We hardly ever went to town." That was the experience of a woman who spent a part of her childhood near the Bristol farm, past Slaughter Pen Curve.

"He had all kinds of groceries," stated another woman "but I mostly remember the candy." A lady who lived at Longtown said that her sons loved Tom Thomasson and loved going to his store for chewing gum and candy "every time they had a nickel in their pocket." A woman who lived closer to the town of Andrews as a girl recalled that she would save pennies in order to buy candy at Tom's store. Tom often gave away free samples to children, even those from neighboring communities who came to shop for their parents or who simply came to visit. Ann Miller Woodford, who grew up in the Happy Top community, reported that she and other neighbors (especially children) would regularly walk across George Lunsford's pasture on their way to Thomasson's store.

In Tom's store, you could find just about anything you needed or wanted in the line of food. He would have commercially canned products and seasonal vegetables he bought from, or traded with, community members. Tom would often accept eggs in barter as well. You could get kerosene for your lamps there. Gene Palmer remembered buying it there. Tom kept a supply in a metal barrel with a hand-cranked pump. Also inside the store were tobacco products to dip, chew or smoke. Occasionally, Thomasson Cash Store stocked an odd item like costume jewelry.

A woman who grew up halfway between Longtown and Main Street at Andrews recalled that her mother would send her up to Thomasson's store to get sewing thread. She did so because the thread was less expensive than in town and because she preferred the brand Tom stocked. The store and a bank of mailboxes beside the main road made Tom Thomasson's house the cynosure of "The Town," even to a stranger.

Tom Thomasson's country store was mostly operated out of house U. It may have been in house T in the earliest years. It is known to have been briefly stationed at house K after that dwelling was purchased by two of Tom's children and their spouses. Tom downsized the store in the late 1950s to early 1960s. His daughter Cora capably continued to operate the business into the late 1960s. Sales slowly dried up as lifestyles changed. A few surviving tax receipts from the era showed sales of $98.00 for the month of July, 1966 and just $66.30 for September of 1967.

Image 6-3: Old sign from store.

*****

One of the first community efforts came to Longtown courtesy of Dr. H. N. Wells. On several early deeds there is mention of a landmark, a small piece of property known by various related names. Formally it was the "Doctor Wells Maple Camp and Spring." Other monikers included "Dr. Wells' old camp" and "Wells' Maple Camp Place." Wells himself referred to the area as "my camp." Its earliest mention by name is from a 1908 document. Subsequent deeds listed the locale as a landmark in property descriptions for many years, even into modern times.

Image 6-4: The above gathering, pictured at Dr. Well's Maple Camp, is believed to be a Methodist Sunday School group. Wells is kneeling at the front, center of the group. Enhancement of the image reveals lettering on the sign "Welcome to the Maple Camp." The photo is estimated to have been taken about 1906 or 1907.

Given Wells' love of the outdoors it is reasonable to conclude that he must have lodged at the Maple Camp property on rustic retreats. There was a small cabin. It is possible that the camp may have also figured loosely into Dr. Wells' vision of a health resort in Cherokee County that never materialized. There is evidence that Wells hosted community groups, such as Sunday school classes, at the retreat (see Image 6-4). Perhaps they came there for picnics, for nature walks or for similar leisurely pursuits. Wells also had a personal and civic fondness for "Leatherwood Lookout" as evidenced by documents from the era. That spot is also mentioned as a landmark on one or two early deeds. A post card from at least as early as 1907 shows a view of "Andrews N. C., from Leather Wood Look Out Mountain." It is likely that Wells commissioned the image and card. It is shown in Image 6-5.

Andrews, N. C., from Leather Wood, Look Out Mountain

Image 6-5: Postcard. The postmark on this copy is 1907. One structure on the photo readers may recognize is the historic F. P Cover home which sits today behind Wilson Street and the railroad tracks. Note the house near the upper right in the photo, behind the tree limbs.

Dr. Wells and his wife Laura seemed to be especially protective of a bountiful water spring on the Maple Camp site. It is one of several major springs on the old Leatherwood property. At least as early as 1907, Wells and others conceived of a system of pipes and catch basins to supply water to the new Andrews City School buildings. A site he identified as "Leatherwood Spring" was to be the primary water reservoir. The Wells Spring, at the Maple Camp Place, was more than a mile away from "School House Hill." Yet, it was in line (with others) to serve as a backup water source if needed. The spring at Dr. Well's old camp is still in private use.

*****

Just at the edge of Longtown, near the Bruce Bristol place and Brady place (house A), members of the Bristol Family maintained a sawmill for a time. Various members of the family participated in the enterprise. Some community historians note that Jack Bristol was an especially integral part of the business. It was at this station where Ray Lunsford apprenticed and learned skills that would help him to establish his own mills at Bryson City, NC and Maryville, TN. Ray and some of his brothers helped to feed a heavy industrial demand for loom shuttles made from durable dogwood timber.

For a while, Billy Palmer had a blacksmith shop at Longtown. He worked across the road from houses B and C which were described in the Longtown tour from the previous chapter. When conditions were right the steady cadence of Palmer's work (*tap tap tap*) could be heard echoing all over Longtown. Palmer's granddaughter Betty Beck Golden recalled pumping the bellows to keep the fire going strong while Mr. Palmer worked. When not helping her grandfather, young Betty assisted her grandmother Sarah Hicks Palmer in the making of lye soap.

Image 6-6: This photo of Billy Palmer (left) and Jim Murray was taken at Santeetlah around 1924. Palmer kept a permanent station for his work, mostly blacksmithing, at Longtown until the family left the settlement in the 1940s. Refer also to Image 5-1.

*****

James Dedrick (J. D.) Harris was born at Flag Pond, in eastern Tennessee, in 1859. He and his family lived in Longtown for many years. Part of what is now known as "Harris Hollow" was the original site for Doctor Wells Maple Camp and Spring. Harris came to the community in 1916. He died in 1933 but his descendants remained for several years.

Dedrick Harris was an incredibly skilled musician. Mr. Harris was to the genre of old time fiddle music as Bill Haley or Fats Domino was to rock music. Much of his musical repertoire was preserved and transmitted through direct instruction and mentoring of various other old time musicians.

J. D. Harris competed in many fiddle competitions. He performed widely and to much acclaim. He was apparently a major draw at political rallies and various other community events throughout the region. In 1924 Harris journeyed to New York to record at Paramount Studios. The resulting three 78 rpm Broadway records, containing six songs, are incredibly rare documents. A steady, swirling rendition of *The Grey Eagle* from that recording session was re-mastered and included in a 2006 anthology from Yazoo Records called *The Stuff that Dreams are made of: The Dead Sea Scrolls of Record Collecting.*

Image 6-7: A selection from the 1924 recording session.

Mr. Harris also played for the Okeh record label in one of legendary Ralph Peer's first field recording sessions. That assembly took place in Asheville, NC in 1925 at the George Vanderbilt Hotel. Sadly, only one song from that session is known to have been mastered for commercial release. *Cackling Hen* was Harris' most widely circulated recording (see Image 6-8).

It has been said that J. D. Harris used a handmade fiddle, fashioned in the 1840s, on some of his recordings. The playing style and tunes he performed were a link to ancient times. Today's historians and old-time music fans are fortunate that the primitive recording industry of the 1920s caught even a tiny shimmer of the immense talent of J. D. Harris.

Image 6-8: Executives at the Okeh record label made a point to note the location of their now historic field recordings at Asheville, NC on the earliest pressings of this J. D. Harris title.

*****

There probably was a fair amount of illicit manufacturing and sale of alcoholic beverages at Longtown over the years. Two men were champions of that art in the 1940s. They sought out cool springs and remote hollows for their craft. Here is a puzzle: The initials of those two men (in alphabetical order) were CEHJLS.

*****

For many years Tom Thomasson's daughter, Ora, sold dairy products from her home. Like so many others in the neighborhood she and her kin maintained a family farm. She had chickens and cows. The family worked, by hand, massive fields of corn at the old Pullium place. In addition to that, they had garden sites closer to their house. Ora was known to preserve blackberry jelly in half-gallon jars to help feed her large family. Her youngest son, Loster, recalled picking blackberries at the head of one of the hollows on the Pullium property. "You didn't cut down any blackberry briars then. You let them grow." He said.

As the number of children living at Ora's house shrank, she was able to sell more and more products to her neighbors and friends. She had a steady stream of loyal customers for her butter, cream and buttermilk. Some of the Jones children, who grew up near the Happytop community, recalled walking across the Lunsford pasture to buy milk products.

"Sweet milk" was the term given to whole milk. Ora sold that as well. Milking was usually done twice daily, in the early morning hours and after supper. In later years electric lights were installed in the barn thanks to a series of wires and extension cords. This helped to make the early shift more convenient. The barn cats usually got the freshest milk, right in their daily pan of food. Ora would sometimes provide them with a quick, playful squirt of milk toward their mouth as she worked.

Ora and her husband George would bring buckets of fresh milk to the enclosed back porch of their home. If any was to be set aside for churning it would be covered with a white cloth and allowed to sit. When the time was right, the stone crocks would be filled with the aged milk. Ora would then plug her electric churn dasher into an accessory receptacle in the ceiling light socket. She had wooden molds for the processed butter. One pressed a decorative daisy print into the round butter pat; another had a pineapple pattern. Sweet milk and butter milk would be poured into quart-sized glass milk bottles, topped with cardboard lids (or in later years poured into heavy half-gallon jars kept from store bought juice) and stored in the "Kelvinator" for customers.

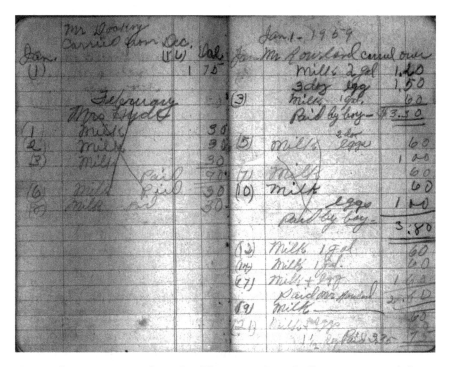

Image 6-9: A pair pages from Ora Thomasson Lunsford's January, 1959 ledger. Note that $3.30 and $1.00 was "paid by [the Rowland] boy" during two visits, one week apart. Mr. Rowland brought in a payment on January 17th. Other customers for the month included the Hyde and Dockery families.

*****

Apart from farming, a number of people at Longtown were able to make at least part of their living off the land. Timber sales took place every few years to help pay taxes. Before the blight struck, people would gather chestnuts in late summer and fall. They were as good as money in local stores. Most of the chestnuts coming off the mountains and hillsides of the region ended in markets in big cities.

Neil Lunsford was an expert outdoorsman. He sold a lot of hides, mostly muskrat, from animals he trapped in nearby streams. Other hides were harvested as well. Mr. Lunsford would allow them to dry and cure on special boards of various sizes which he kept for that purpose.

Neil Lunsford and others, notably Mr. Bob Rogers, were skilled ginseng hunters. In the earliest years not too many people in the area knew much about ginseng. The market for that plant was just not established in the United States. Local people recognized ginseng and some used it in herbal medicines. But the idea of digging massive quantities for sale was unheard of. Another herb, goldenseal, was the lucrative prize. For many decades the Pullium, Thomasson and Lunsford families nursed and cultivated a remnant population of goldenseal on Pullium/Lunsford land. They even created artificial shade for the plants during the harshest days of summer after a forest clear cut. On occasion, spare plants would be sold to the herbal medicine trade. Today, the tables are turned. Hardly anyone even knows what goldenseal is. Ginseng is the highly sought after herb of the mountains.

Sometimes local residents, particularly children, would catch "spring lizards" (actually salamanders) to sell as fish bait. The streams at Longtown once had small populations of minnows. The overzealous harvesting of those for bait accounts for their demise.

The biologist Jesse Nicholls would sometimes pass through to buy biological specimens, such as salamanders, for research. He was known to collect bats as well. A war-era project had him harvesting poison snakes for preparation of snake bite antivenom. In his busiest years Mr. Nicholls' field work netted him payments that approached ten thousand dollars.

*****

For a few years, Longtown resident Catharine Morton supplemented her retirement with animal husbandry. As previously noted, Miss Morton taught school in Andrews for many terms. Several adults referred to her as "Granny Morton" as a term of endearment in her later years. Miss Catharine Morton would breed, raise and sell small mammals such as guinea pigs and rabbits. Most of the animals were used in scientific research. Miss Morton would sell them by the hundreds. Universities such as Duke and the University of Tennessee were among her customers.

*****

A few people who lived at Longtown were able to work out of their homes on a limited basis. These jobs mostly helped to bring extra income into the households. John Henry Thomasson, Tom's son, would occasionally sell nursery plants. He would take orders and sometimes travel door-to-door. It is a safe bet that many of the large English boxwoods in our region passed through John Henry's hands. He was also skilled at leather crafts. He made a number of purses and wallets which he sometimes sold.

John Henry's brother, Fulton, did intermittent work as a salesman in his life. He would take orders for clothing and shoes to help pay for college. Later in his life, he worked as an advertising salesman for the AD-CRAFT Line. Fulton took a great deal of pleasure in giving away extra samples of pencils, pens and glossy color art work to children as he queried them about their plans for college. AD-CRAFT also offered things like thermometers and calendars which they could custom produce for any business in need of good advertising paraphernalia.

Fulton Thomasson should get much more credit than he has received for work to establish adult educational options in our region. Mr. Thomasson spent hours going door-to-door, recording pledges and carrying petitions. His pitch for higher learning in our region was as earnest and compelling as that of any salesman hocking any wares. Fulton Thomasson's niece, Leila, remembers typing a flurry of correspondence to assist Fulton in his mission.

"Aunt Jenny" Lunsford was one of the few women of the community who found an opportunity for steady, paying work in her home. Not too many details are remembered about the yarn factory at Andrews which engaged her. A gentleman from the factory would bring unprocessed yarn to the Lunsford house on a predictable schedule. He would pick up the neatly wound yarn skeins from the previous visit and return them to the old barn which housed the facility.

*****

"Miss Ruth and Miss Charlotte were the missionaries who started that Sunday school over there." So begins most of the stories from people who were children at Longtown during the 1940s. It is true that Longtown once had its own church.

Charlotte Bishop and Ruth Gruber moved into the old Nichols place (house K, which many will remember as the Fulton Thomasson home) and began their operations by having prayer meetings and afternoon Sunday school in the early to mid 1940s. One of the Lunsford girls, Tommie, recalled that the ladies maintained one private room at the house and that the remainder of the rooms was devoted to Sunday school classes. "They had a big following," she said. "We would go to their Sunday school in the afternoons and our own church in the morning. So, we went to Sunday school twice in a day." Another woman recalled that Miss Ruth and Miss Charlotte came by to invite her family to church services not too long after they moved to Andrews. She was a young girl at the time and that invitation has remained vivid in her memory.

Image 6-10: Cora Lee Buchanan, Hazel Lunsford, Nannie Belle Buchanan and Wayne Lunsford (all in their Sunday clothes) pose in front of Longtown Chapel. Note their canine companion.

Some people called Bishop and Gruber's Methodist-leaning establishment "Longtown Chapel." The missionaries, along with Gladys Tubbs, several members of the Matheson family and many others from the local community helped to start the house of worship which eventually morphed into the Andrews Free Methodist Church. It occupied a building along Sixth Street in Andrews. That building has since been demolished. Another noteworthy piece of Longtown history associated with the church is the fact that a small residence situated behind house A (the Brady place, see Image 5-1) once served as the parsonage for the Andrews Free Methodist Church. In later years that house and property were absorbed into the Brady land.

Image 6-11: The Nichols-Thomasson house. This structure, house K, served myriad purposes including family home, rental home, store site and church. John Henry Thomasson's boxwoods lined the downstairs front porch.

Image 6-12: Friends Edith Raxter and Stella Mae Gregory let the children Loster & Leila Lunsford, and Jane Gregory, enjoy a buggy ride.

Tom Thomasson

In Memory of James
Who Passed Away January 2, 1956

For Mrs. Griffith

God for some great reason
Has taken James away
A shock indeed to everyone
Perhaps he met foul play

He was our good neighbor
When he saw a friend in need
He would quickly stop his job
To do that friend a deed

He kept himself well posted
And knew just how to live
If anyone offended him
He was willing to forgive

Indeed a fine converser
He spoke his English well
In every conversation
Had something good to tell

So kind and noble hearted
He had a host of friends
But left his home and loved ones
His country to defend

Loyal to his captain
Doolittle was his name
He cited all his comrades
To James' deeds of fame

A message of importance
By James he'd always send
He told all his buddies
On James he could depend

His aim was to protect us
From Mussolini's hand
And save our lovely nation
From Hitler's awful band

A noble shell-shocked soldier
Who served his country well
And helped protect our nation
From Adolph Hitler's hell

He dearly loved his mother
He loved his wife as well
But how he loved his baby girl
No human tongue can tell

Note: James Arthur Griffith was the son of Arthur and Ezra Griffith. During World War II he served in the Military Police in the US Army. He was the husband of Mae Lunsford.

Tom Thomasson

Mrs. Thomasson's Family Dinner

Big Mamma gave us dinner. She thought she would be smart
She loves to feed the children. She wants to do her part
We had a splendid dinner, at her little hotel
She fed half of Longtown, as near as we could tell

'twas fine to see Big Mamma shaking her sides around
Looking for the children, 'til every one was found
She saw them each one seated before she ate a bite
To give these children dinner was surely her delight

Leila was the sponsor. She knows exactly how
She served chicken and dumplings, and sweet potato pie
They brought in lots of "rashins" to help the dinner out
Of course they would have brought more, but they were nearly out

We ate up all the chicken. We ate up all the jam
We ate and ate and ate, as long as we could stand
They knocked us pretty hard, but worse it could have been
Guess we will even up with them before the next weekend

It Could have Been Worse

The last day of November,
Nineteen and thirty six
Was a day of much surprise
When Garland and I mixed

He drew his gun right on me
I backed off like a fool
Until I got a slight chance
I snatched it calm and cool

It was a bad occasion
King Alcohol stepped in
And made my neighbor crazy
I swore he would not win

The Lord was surely with us
In iron rod and gun
We had an awful tussle
For some folks it was fun

Although I was sixty-five
I felt like I was young
I did everything I could
From when it first begun

I used every brain I had
To hold him very tight
I did not mean to hurt him much
But meant to have him tied

Perhaps I saved his own wife
Perhaps his baby dear
Perhaps I saved his own life
From the electric chair

He told me when he sobered
With whiskey he was done
He pledged to me his honor
For all his time to come

He asked of me forgiveness
What more could I then say
Than "Seventy – times -- seven"
He quit whiskey that day

He thanked me for my efforts
To save his wife and child
He praised me for all I did
While he was whiskey wild

He is now an abstainer
A man that is worthwhile
A real example for our boys
Instead of being wild

Longtown Blues

Mama I am lonely here
Daddy there's no one to cheer
I am going to the farm
Where there is fields of hay and corn

Chorus: I am leaving Longtown soon. I can't stand these weary blues

Won't that be a jubilee?
When from Longtown I am free
In the fields of waving grain
He will call me by my name

Chorus: I am leaving Longtown soon. I can't stand these weary blues

We will plant and we will sow
We will reap and we will mow
You'll be lonely over here
We'll be happy over there

Chorus: I am leaving Longtown soon. I can't stand these weary blues

You can find us if you will
In the cottage by the mill
We'll be happy, happy still
In the village on the hill

Chorus: I am leaving Longtown soon. I can't stand these weary blues

You will miss me when I'm gone
While the years roll on, roll on
Goodbye Mama I am gone
Farewell Daddy I am gone

Chorus: I am leaving Longtown soon. I can't stand these weary blues. I
am leaving Longtown soon. I can't stand these weary blues

Chapter 7

Around Andrews

"The Town" (Tom's own neighborhood) was detailed in Chapters Five and Six. "The Town" was situated less than one mile from the official downtown section of Andrews, North Carolina. Tom made regular trips into Andrews for various purposes. He would visit people along the way or he would catch up with their lives by speaking to mutual acquaintances. Newspapers and barber shop gossip were also sources of knowledge about local happenings.

Narratives concerning a number of interesting people and events from Andrews were preserved by Tom's pencil and tablet. Sometimes he paid tribute to entire families or to the splendid scenery. He was so impressed with a neighbor's landscaping skills that he poetized *Hancock Davis Arboretum*. Mr. Davis, by the way, was a local pharmacist who lived with his family (all friends to Tom's extended family) along the way to town.

At least two creations from this chapter were published in the town paper, which Tom inexplicably called "The Andrews Times." One concerned the great Cherokee leader known to history as "Junaluska." Andrews, NC certainly does not have a monopoly on Junaluska's legacy, as he traveled extensively and played a major role in numerous historical events. Tom's tribute to him is included in this chapter because Junaluska identified strongly with the area (and with Graham County) as a home site. A stream, Junaluska Creek, is named for him. *The Ferebee Maple Park* celebrates a public picnic area and playground, less than a mile from Tom Thomasson's home, secured for Andrews by Percy B. Ferebee. Mr.

Ferebee's impact on Andrews, as well as the entire western North Carolina region and beyond is strongly reverberating many years after his death.

Tom Thomasson had a noteworthy role in Andrews and neighboring communities as well. His daughter Cora described him as a "singing leader." He would teach rudiments or fine details of music to any agreeable pupil. Most of the lessons were very informal but he did occasionally organize what could best be called a subscription school. Every one of Tom Thomasson's children and grandchildren knew the basics. All three daughters could play the pump organ and piano. Cora was especially practiced on the organ.

One of Tom's favorite pastimes was to gather relatives, friends, neighbors and all willing souls into a type of gospel choir then known as a "Banner Class." Such classes were usually composed of members of a particular church or a particular community. There were also age-based or gender-based assemblages in some locales. From Image 7-1 note that the words "Longtown Jr. Singing Class" had been printed across a surviving copy of James D. Vaughn's *Bells of Heaven* hymnal. The various singing classes would not only practice religiously (pun intended) but they would also go up against other classes for a "banner." The banner was the modest equivalent of a blue ribbon or trophy among the gospel singers who competed.

"You had to sing too brother," noted Tom's daughter Ora. "If you didn't get it right you had to do it over." Cora added in recollection that "We sung down here at the school house, that school house that burned down. We got the banner there and we got the junior banner there too. We sung up at Valley River Church one time and got the banner there."

More often than not, Cora accompanied the group on piano and sang as well. Lillian Love noted that it was not unusual for cheering to break out as the Longtown Banner classes passed by in a car on their way to a competition.

David Young is one of many people who saw Tom Thomasson's banner classes participate in contests. He noted that the larger banner competitions could turn into all-day events in Andrews and nearby towns. He remembers watching in the Andrews High School auditorium. The event was sponsored by the Farmer's Federation of North Carolina. James G. K. McClure and others were important in founding that group. One of the refreshments offered during the banner competition was large watermelons, sliced with the dull side of a handsaw. Great crowds came to enjoy the music, catch up on local happenings and visit with friends.

Image 7-1: Close up of hymnal cover.

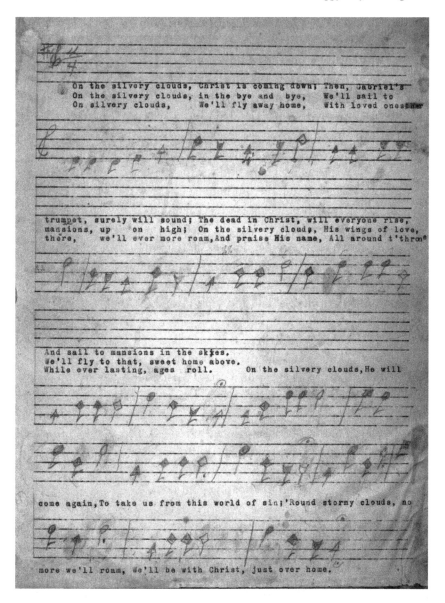

Image 7-2: Handwritten shape notes from an original hymn composed by Tom Thomasson are shown above. His music pupils would have studied and sung from notation similar to this. Complete lyrics to the hymn *On the Silvery Clouds* are presented in Chapter 10.

Our Scenic Assets

Andrews is a splendid town
With scenic assets all around
Some of the assets here that pay
Are marble quarries, blue and gray

Our valley here is one great chain
With fields of corn and waving grain
Scenic resorts here at home
The half of which has not been told

We see the mines de Soto dug
Here where the mountains round us hug
So rich in iron and precious gold
With marble, talc and useful stone

Now if you wish to take a stroll
Wade down the river o'er the shole
Great pockets there we have been told
Are often found with sparkling gold

The river bed o'er lain with stone
Nature through the ages with sand has worn
Great cavities, pockets or holes
To gather up the floating gold

Now if you wish to take a hike
You can quickly see great sights
By going up McClelland's Creek
But you will find the mountain steep

Stop at the quarry on your way
To see how nature stored away
The builders' stones, most any length,
Of scantlings, blocks and fancy planks

There's nothing finer anywhere
There's nothing with these rocks compare
A mountain high with fancy slabs
The world is needing mighty bad

It's scenic here to see indeed
The pretty rocks the builder needs
With seams complete that nature made
And on the mountain for us laid

The slabs we use to decorate
Our walls and steps and pretty gates
The scraps we use on walks of sport
Around our pretty tennis courts

Now we will climb the mountain steep
To view the balds and pretty peaks
When we have reached the county line
The famous tower we will climb

We'll view the landscape o'er and o'er
We'll watch the eagle 'round us soar
With pride we now are looking down
At scenic assets of our town

Now from this tour we soon will fly
Across the valley very high
Around our town we too will soar
And look our scenic assets o'er

Junaluska

Junaluska, we have been told
Was chief of many tribes of old
A better chief could not be found
He always meant to hold his ground

His name-sake creek flows through our town
By ancient camps and pretty mounds
Perpetuating Juna's name
And where he gained his noted fame

General Jackson, Juna's friend
By vicious tribes had been condemned
'twas he who kept the sneak attack
From angry Creeks close on his tracks

Small in stature but large in mind
A better friend could not be found
Exile to tribes was then proclaimed
But Junaluska still remained

Up to the White House Juna trod
To free his tribes from exile gods
He gained some land he called his own
Where all his tribe desired to roam

Then to the mountains Juna fled
To dry the tears of those he led
Determined his hunting ground to roam
Around the peaks of his dear home

He led the way with tomahawk
From duty he would never balk
He was as brave as any lion
A failure never crossed his mind

The ancient camp of Juna's pride
A favored spot of all his tribe
Surrounded by mountain sides
That marked the place poor Juna died

Juna's tribe we have been told
Wrapped him up in his fur clothes
And carried him around the trails
For many lonely nights and days

O'er the hills and trails they wound
To find a happy hunting ground
They buried him high on a hill
Above the town of Robbinsville

The little town built modern trails
And pretty steps up to his grave
Where many tribes come every year
To shed for him a weeping tear

Take Your Home Paper

Why not take the "Andrews Times" to help the printer out?
A town without a paper is almost out of sight
We have a splendid county. We have a splendid town
Chock-full of splendid people who ought to take the *Times*

If we will boost our paper, then we will boost our town
Now let's turn in the happenings, from all the country 'round
Now take the Andrews paper. Put in a few more ads
We'll soon have the best paper our town has ever had

Note: In addition to the currently printed "Andrews Journal," at least two other newspapers including "Andrews" in their titles are known historically. These are the "Andrews Record" and the "Andrews Sun." Whether the "Andrews Times" was an actual periodical is not known. It may have been used by Tom Thomasson as a nickname for any of these local papers.

The Ferebee Maple Park

November 1, 1950

This park – a triangle, three square lot;
the prettiest place that we have got
It helps to form the five points street,
that leads to all our vales and peaks
Indeed it was an abrupt lot,
but now it is our beauty spot
Surrounded by three lovely streets,
this Ferebee gave us all for keeps

It is equipped with seats and swings,
and many other pretty things
It amuses tourists one and all,
to hear the children laugh and squall
This park once strewn with rustic stones,
surrounded now with pretty homes
Is one of our most lovely scenes,
with suits of purple, red and green

We use this park to meditate,
when we come home both soon and late
The cooling shades refresh our minds
and keep our problems all in line
The maple trees so large and tall,
invite the children one and all
To chase the leaves like butterflies,
as they fly from toward the skies

Protect our rustic maple trees.
Protect them for the honey bees
Protect them for their pretty leaves;
from traffic's trouble, they relieve
Protect them for the flocks and herds.
Protect them for the singing birds
For to the twigs they carefully cling,
most every day to chirp and sing

Protect those trees from year to year,
for Mother Nature put them here
The owner gave them to our town.
A better gift could not be found
Protect we say the maple trees.
Protect them for the evening breeze
Protect them for their cooling shades,
'cause God for us those trees have made

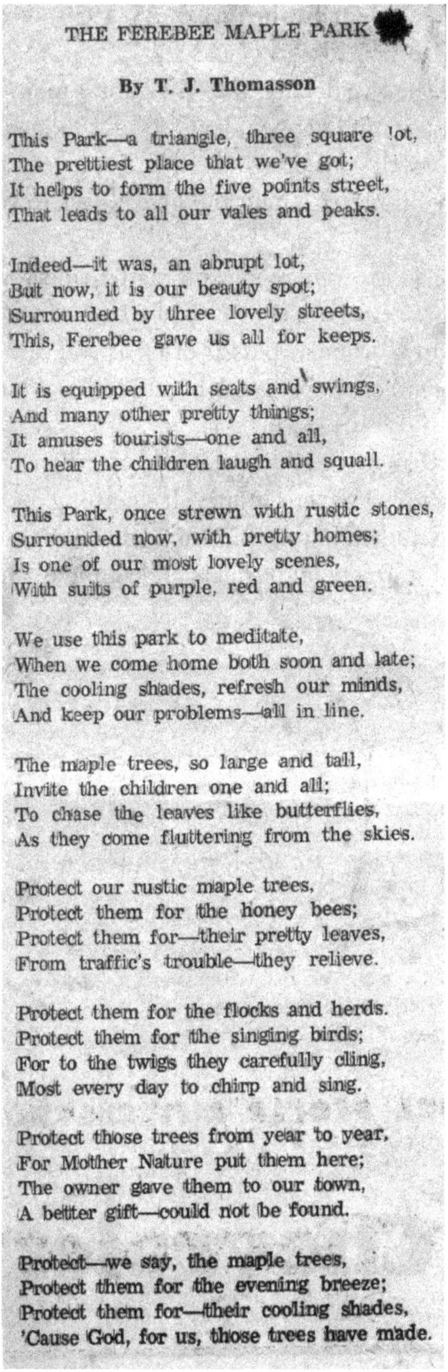

THE FEREBEE MAPLE PARK

By T. J. Thomasson

This Park—a triangle, three square lot,
The prettiest place that we've got;
It helps to form the five points street,
That leads to all our vales and peaks.

Indeed—it was, an abrupt lot,
But now, it is our beauty spot;
Surrounded by three lovely streets,
This, Ferebee gave us all for keeps.

It is equipped with seats and swings,
And many other pretty things;
It amuses tourists—one and all,
To hear the children laugh and squall.

This Park, once strewn with rustic stones,
Surrounded now, with pretty homes;
Is one of our most lovely scenes,
With suits of purple, red and green.

We use this park to meditate,
When we come home both soon and late;
The cooling shades, refresh our minds,
And keep our problems—all in line.

The maple trees, so large and tall,
Invite the children one and all;
To chase the leaves like butterflies,
As they come fluttering from the skies.

Protect our rustic maple trees,
Protect them for the honey bees;
Protect them for—their pretty leaves,
From traffic's trouble—they relieve.

Protect them for the flocks and herds.
Protect them for the singing birds;
For to the twigs they carefully cling,
Most every day to chirp and sing.

Protect those trees from year to year,
For Mother Nature put them here;
The owner gave them to our town,
A better gift—could not be found.

Protect—we say, the maple trees,
Protect them for the evening breeze;
Protect them for—their cooling shades,
'Cause God, for us, those trees have made.

Image 7-3: Newspaper clipping of *The Ferebee Maple Park.*

Dear Junior: April 25, 1934

I received the five dollars. It to the bank I took
If anything should happen, you'll find it in my book
It was very well considered, the best thing you could do
You know I'll keep it safely and give it back to you

That's the way to save money no matter who you are
So when we get a surplus, we can buy a nice new car
Just send in all your surplus as often as you can
And then you cannot waste it because it's not on hand

Just buy what you really need and that will be enough
It's wrong to waste your money. It's nothing else but stuff
If you had all you've wasted, you could be at your ease
You could start a good business and run it as you please

The Famous Ratterree Family

We are thinking very kindly of the famous Ratterree braves
Especially of their captain who crossed the roaring seas
The are a model family, for people all around
No better folks in common can anywhere be found

The father and the mother, so kind to everyone
The confidence of neighbors, most surely they have won
There are no better neighbors. They're good to one and all
In sickness or misfortune, they help at every call

The father -- a promoter, to boys and girls in school
With thirty years of teaching, he knows his P's and Q's
He is an educator, no matter where he goes
Education he's promoted, so much that no one knows

The best of all they're workers for Christ, the mighty one
No doubt they both were praying for Captain James, their son
That he might fill his missions o'er seas and dangerous guns
And then return home safely when victory there was won

We're glad their prayers were answered and James is back in school
To finish up his college work and other work then choose
We'd like to meet that captain. We know he's done much good
With fifty-three safe missions, there's very few that could

Our Hunter's Guide Passed Away January 5, 1957

Paul Franklin, a mountain lover,
has just gone from us away
To wait for all his loved ones
'till the debt of death they pay
It was indeed an awful shock
as everyone can tell
But we must submit to God's will
because he doeth all things well

Paul was a mountain genius,
knowing most every mountain trail
He always led his comrades
to abundant fields of game
Familiar with the Great Smokies,
from Hazel Creek to Clingman's Dome
He led his band of sportsmen
to their paradise of goal

He was kind and noble hearted,
chock-full of jokes and fun
With many deeds of kindness
for every single one
We are lonely, Oh! so lonely
since he went from us away
But we know that we can only
look to God for help each day

His active life on Earth is o're
but his kind words and deeds live on
His soul has flown to Heaven's shore
to be with loved ones evermore
Our circle here is now broken
we feel so sad and lonely here
But we must trust the promise spoken.
Oh! may it not be broken there

Note: In addition to being a friend of the Thomasson family, Paul Franklin was the brother of Glenna (Polly) Franklin who was Tom Thomasson's daughter-in-law. She was married to T. J Thomasson Jr.

A Tribute to Our Preacher

God sent a gracious preacher
from somewhere in the state
To Christianize our people
before it was too late

He always talked religion
just everywhere he went
And that is why we believe
that he to us was sent

He doesn't fail when praying
for all those who are lost
To lead folks right to Jesus
without one cent of cost

He is a gallant speaker
with language plain and clear
He quotes to us the scripture
that fills our hearts with cheer

He is a splendid mixer
and never waits too late
To get folks all united
who for the future wait

He always brings a message
of Christ's eternal love
To all his congregation
with power from above

We all are mighty thankful
God sent him back this way
To harmonize our people
by teaching night and day

He is our dear preacher
the one we all adore
May he live long and happy
and God his needs restore

And when this short life is over
in the sweet by and by
we trust that we will meet him
above the starry sky

To Oma Carver Almond

A poor washer woman was left with four little girls to feed, clothe and educate.

To Oma Carver Almond was left four little girls
She worked and strove to teach them, they were her only pearls
A noble heart this mother had, though she was very poor
To labor she would leave her home, to feed her precious four

She was a model mother, with Carlee by her side
To assist in all her efforts and help for them provide
Perhaps her way looked gloomy when Carlee from her had gone
But she picked up new courage and then kept pressing on

Now she must look to Bessie who, no doubt, obeys her rules
For Mildred and Reathel are each one still in school
To educate her children, it seemed was her great pride
That when she shall have left them, they'll be above the tide

To keep them food and clothing, she did a mother's part
To teach and educate them, was then next to her heart
I'm sure that over Jordan, beyond the rolling tide
She'll receive a great reward and with the good abide

Such women should be happy while others take their rest
Their time is swiftly coming, when they'll be Heaven's guests
Now may her circle not be broken when this toilsome life is o'er
But may they all be gathered on that happy golden shore

More Truth than Poetry

I credit Mr. Tillitt with much of my success
For he was optimistic and gave the very best
I met him in his kitchen. His lunch he had to fix
His wife was somewhere teaching. We then our ideas mixed

I told him I was anxious to work my way through school
He gave me consolation by laying out some rules
He said it took ambition, also a lot of pep
"Stick – um – tight" and resolutions to education get

You appeared against my daddy and his bank note you won
For the Manufactures Bank that was a handsome sum
I think you did your duty although it was not just
To your clients you must be true or you, they could not trust

Now I am selling garments. I'm also selling shoes
I've got to make some money to help me out in school
I thank you for your counsel. I'll do my very best
To follow your instructions; I'll do as you request

I made good on all my subjects in all the Andrews High
I finally graduated. By some means I got by.
When I had finished high school to college I was bent
I didn't know what to do. I didn't have a cent

I know Dad would have sent me if I had asked him to
But I somewhat peculiar just thought I'd make it through
He always loaned me money. He knew I'd pay him back
He said 'twas better for me if I could make the hike

I talked to Mr. Tillitt. He said "Don't be alarmed."
I worked out a six weeks course, between the railroad irons
He said "Now go to college to Nashville, Tennessee."
I went to the Peabody. It was a job for me

It was a proposition so far away from home
With very little money but I was not alone
It was a splendid city, I'd never seen about
I worked at the cafeteria to help my board bill out

'twas then to Johnson City, for a term I was bent
So when I passed my subjects, I didn't have a cent
'twas up to me to study just how I would get back
I wasn't long deciding that I would just hitch-hike

Up on North Carolina I now must graduate
At our University right in my native state
When I was graduated I began to look around
The very books, I didn't know were the biggest books I found

Note: This is an unusual poem, apparently written by Tom Thomasson from the perspective of his son Fulton. Fulton may have composed it himself. Details from the piece closely match entries from Fulton Thomasson's curriculum vitae. As unusual as it sounds today, Fulton actually completed substantial college work, and taught school for four years, before graduating high school. A 1925 letter from F. C. Nye, the Andrews School District Superintendent, notes Fulton's upcoming graduation and his experience as a professional educator. At this time Fulton would have been almost 27 years of age. The reference in the verses to "Johnson City" reflects Fulton's attendance at East Tennessee State Teacher's College. Mr. D. Howard Tillitt was a prominent citizen of Andrews who lived in a house at the intersection of Cherry and Aquone Streets. He was an attorney and took much interest in the welfare of others. Tillitt served briefly as mayor of Andrews. In later years someone recalled that he was of great assistance in getting certain sidewalks installed in town. His wife was an educator. Following Mr. Tillitt's death in 1940, his family left the area.

The Tannery Line Blues

Mama I am leaving soon
I can't stand these tannery blues
I will leave the tannery line
I'll go with that pal of mine

Chorus: I will leave the tannery soon. I can't stand these tannery blues.

I will go with "Tooter Bill"
He will take me, yes he will
He's my "Tooter" I'm his "Vine"
We'll be happy all the time

Chorus: I will leave the tannery soon. I can't stand these tannery blues.

We will drive away out west
Where they say that times are best
You can find us if you will
We will stop at Granite Mills

Chorus: I will leave the tannery soon. I can't stand these tannery blues.

We will drive out to our farm
Where there's fields of hay and corn
You can see us from your train
'round our fields of waving grain

Chorus: I will leave the tannery soon. I can't stand these tannery blues.

Goodbye daddy, goodbye dear
From you all we hope to hear
Write me Norma; write me Dill
Send in care of Granite Mill.

Chorus: I will leave the tannery soon. I can't stand these tannery blues.

Note: The Andrews Tanning Company *(previously called the "F. P. Cover &* Sons Tannery)" *provides the backdrop for this song. Mr. Lono William Pullium was sometimes called "Tooter Bill." The lady who would become his wife was Vinie Lunsford. In the song, she is called "Vine." In the final lines of the song "Norma and Dill" reference Dillie and Norma Truett Lunsford.*

Hancock Davis Arboretum

December 11, 1950

An attractive arboretum of native scenic trees
With many pretty flowers, for the humming of the bees
The shrubbery is so well arranged, it attracts the tourists' eye
They look like mountain chains to all the passersby

Here laurels hide the ugly spots, rhododendrons with them share.
Sweet fragrance from the roses fill all the atmosphere
Nightingales perch on the trees as if talking to their mates
"Away down in this beauty spot for you I watch and wait"

A better place could not be found for boys to hide and seek
An ideal spot indeed, it never could be beat.
Every tree is placed just right around the pool and oak
We linger here and listen; to hear the bullfrog croak

Goldfish dart across the pool to see who is coming next
Looks like they are playing school or which can beat the rest
A haven for the butterflies; for hummingbirds and bees
They sip away the honey from the blooming plants and trees

Each plant has its own natural form and its peculiar bloom
With many colors and designs and many sweet perfumes
The lilac and the daisies are standing all upright
With nature's decorations it is a pretty sight

This completes a model home, surrounded by selected trees
That will lull you off to sleep by the twittering of the leaves
This is a fine example for all the folks around
To beautify their own homes and make their village shine

Note: Mr. Davis was a druggist in the town of Andrews NC. His home was about halfway between Tom Thomasson's house and the business section of Andrews, North Carolina.

Dr. Jack Mintz, Our Barber

Dr. Mintz is our barber
and our veterinarian too
If you'll give him half a chance,
you'll see that this is true

A face and head specialist,
as all barbers should be
He trims the hair up nicely,
as everyone can see

Dr. Mintz is most attractive.
He's six feet, five inches tall.
When you come to Andrews,
be sure on him to call

You will know this handsome doctor,
his eyes are sparking bright
And you'll always see him smiling,
his teeth are pearly white

A veterinarian specialist,
also of face and head
He serves every application
before he goes to bed

Don't fail to see this doctor.
He is full of truth and grace.
He will make your hair look pretty
and rub the wrinkles from your face

He works at "Parker's Barbershop."
He's at the first chair.
Climb up and hear him clatter.
He'll fill your heart with cheer

You'll see he is a specialist.
He never leaves a gap
If you will try out Dr. Mintz,
I'm sure you will come back

When his work days are over,
he hurries home to see
His pretty baby Stephen
and his darling, Sweet Marie

To Stella Mae: December 11, 1940; Andrews NC

I'll tell you now you've got me skinned,
so I can only laugh and grin
The plant is gone and milky too,
but I am sure we'll all get through
It may be best to look around
that it did not come to our town
If it had the German spy,
might have bummed us from near the sky

Our town is growing any way;
we can feel it now most every day
From Topton down the great highway,
the "dam men" come in every day
The City Hall's no little thing,
we're sure that work will soon begin
Then I will have to build some tents;
I've got no more houses now for rent

I gave my renters all a raise;
thirteen is all Tom Cotter pays
The Wilson House is not so clean,
I let it go for just fifteen
I am now seventy years young;
chock-full of pep but not much fun
Write me again, don't wait so long;
Jane and Jacky's great grandfather Tom

*Note: This poem includes local, national and global history as well as some
rare use of figurative language by Tom Thomasson. "The plant" refers to the
P. F. Cover & Sons Tannery which had recently been taken under a new
management with scaled back operations. The "dam men" were employees of
the Utah Construction Company who were building the Nantahala Dam.
The company ran buses from Andrews and nearby towns to take workers to
and from the construction site. Around this time Andrews also began to erect
the City Hall building on what is now Main Street. The United States was
coerced to enter World War II nearly one year from the date on which this poem
was written. A number of events leading to our country's official declaration*

of war was likely on the minds of people during the previous months. In the local language a bomb or a bombing was a "bum." The past tense of "bum" was "bummed." In the opening line of the piece Tom speaks of being "skinned." That term had multiple meanings including being cheated, embarrassed or outdone. Also, one spoke of being skinned when they were the recipient of a prank.

A Greater Andrews: 2/15/1951

A greater Andrews now is born;
'twill make the wheels roll on and on
Long predicted but now 'tis real,
the factory site is now a deal
Here on a plateau, east of town,
a better site could not be found
Surrounded by the mountains high
that seem to be kissing the sky
The scenery 'round this site is grand,
the mountain peaks and level lands
Should cause more folks to come and see
where many factories ought to be
A health resort for everyone
who wants pure air and radiant sun
With fragrance sweet and cooling shade,
that God for all of us has made
There's babbling brooks and bubbling springs,
there's speckled trout and birds to sing
There's flowers for the honey bee.
There's chattering squirrels up in the trees
Our sponsors Percy, Bill and Ted
will still proceed to look ahead
To place more plants on other knolls
until we know we've reached the goal
We must solicit other plants,
to locate here they take no chance
'twill help them out and help our town;
we want more factories all around
Our folks respond to every call
with one accord we do it all
Not very much do we withhold
but split the hair to gain the goal
Here now we think the tourists will light
to see our parks and fancy sites
We hear the echoes day and night
and know our goal is now in sight

Our boys and girls all want to work;
from labor, clean, they never shirk
"A dollar here at home" they say,
"Is more than two so far away."
So now they will not have to roam
for jobs so far away from home
Demand for labor now is great,
so we will not have long to wait
Ten thousand dollars, so they say,
will be the average weekly pay
This handsome sum will help us all
to meet our country's mammoth call
Relax your bodies and your minds
and be out there in ample time
Thanks to our sponsors, others too,
who helped our dreams all to come true

Note: The agreement to establish Berkshire Knitting Mill at Andrews NC was documented by Tom Thomasson as shown above. Local residents usually referred to the factory as "Berkshire." It was formally opened in about 1952 and focused mostly on hosiery. The building still stands and was home to other manufacturing firms in later years.

Andrews Dress Factory

June 20, 1956 while vacationing at Paducah, KY

Thanks to Mr. Owenby
and thanks to all his staff
For locating here in Andrews,
which has raised our standard half
A better site could not be found
than the center of our town
With ideal parking ground
and anxious "seamsters" all around

All the girls are full of pep,
cheered up with extra pay
Instructed by kindhearted folks,
as they skip about each day
The Tankersleys and Ledford;
Johnnie, Howell and Bill,
Have got a factory going
that gives the girls a thrill

It is nice to see them sewing,
they twist about real quick
To fix the dresses pretty
and make them all to fit
Another factory we do need,
to employ the women's men
They could add their pay together
and save some money then

A few more busy factories,
to help prize up our town
Will make Andrews the center,
for many miles around
A health resort and scenery grand,
with mountain peaks and rolling land
Should cause more folks to come and see
where many factories ought to be

There's babbling brooks and bubbling springs.
There's speckle trout and birds to sing
There's flowers for the honey bees.
There's chattering squirrels up in the trees
The hemlock, spruce and native pine,
sing through the breeze a welcome chime
Come on good people, come and see,
five thousand feet above the sea

Note: Tom Thomasson's daughter, Cora, was an early employee of what she called "the dress place" when it was located along Locust Street; less than a mile from Tom's home. That structure has been known locally as the "Firestone Building." The parent company for the dress factory, Owenby Manufacturing, was based in Georgia. They once had two larger factories in simultaneous operation in Andrews.

Chapter 8

Around the Region

COMMENTARY: Chapter Introduction

You don't spend decades of your life running country stores, teaching school, attending church, participating in lodge meetings and being involved in other social events without getting to know a lot of people. So was the case with Tom Thomasson. From a geographic standpoint many of his poetic works focusing on Andrews, Peachtree and Bryson City have already been presented in previous chapters. This chapter will bring other people and places of the western North Carolina, eastern Tennessee and northern Georgia region into the limelight.

Cars, buses, trains and fast walking sticks could help Tom Thomasson make journeys throughout the region surrounding his home. Newspapers, postcards and word of mouth helped to keep him updated about the regional goings on. He would often take day trips with his family or go on short vacations to visit relatives, see friends and take in the sights. Often his children or grandchildren would write the news to him from areas where they worked or lived. Perhaps he got some ideas for poems from those letters or from personal accounts conveyed to him in conversation.

Narratives like *Our Mountains, Echoes around the Great Smokies* and *Blowing Springs* do a good job in reflecting Tom's appreciation for the natural beauty around him. Pieces such as *The Coleman Dam Site, Park to Park Way, Tapoco* and *Parkview Service Station* are striking, poetic snapshots that capture moments of the past in a way no camera could have. An event as insignificant to the outside world as the consolidation of rural school houses draws the reader with urgent curiosity to a chronicle called

Canada, North Carolina. That poem is set in Jackson County, NC as is its sister piece *Our Canadian Mountains.*

No collection of Thomasson poetry would be finished without inclusion of tribute pieces to departed friends or neighbors. *In Memory of Dr. W. C. Mason* fills that slot nicely. Other important figures in regional history are also included in the poems comprising this chapter.

Dear Cora: August 28, 1934

You asked about our flowers and all about our health
Our flowers are our pleasures. Our children is our wealth
You ought to see them shining along our rustic wall
They're scenic in their beauty for every one that calls

I'm just now back from Peachtree. You know my health is good
I walked across to Marble, quick as anybody could
I would have walked to Andrews if I had wanted to
Not being in a hurry, I rode the train on through

I found them fine and dandy. T. J. was right in school
I'm sure he has decided to be no little fool
I hope you have decided which place you'd rather live
Your place or up at Cathy's, the other to Math I'll give

Note: During the time period in which this postcard poem was written, Tom's teenage son was at school and his daughter Cora had moved away with her husband and family to find work. The two exchanged a series of letters discussing which house Cora would occupy when she came back to Andrews to live. The Cathy family lived near Tom. The identity of "Math" (a regionally common nickname for Matthew) is not known.

Our Mountains

Here in western North Carolina
Our mountains are our greatest pride
In our spruce and laurel jungles
Where many beasts and varmints hide

Here too are our great Smokies
Which are the pride of our great state
While climbing to its summits
We find the scenery very great

Two hundred thousand acres strong
To this nation now belongs
Six hundred miles of trickling streams
With babbling books this area drains

The forests here of virgin trees
With scores of ferns and buzzing bees
Great meadows too of waving grass
Are often seen up near the crests

When we have reached the Smoky crest
We look then down into the west
Then looking up with glimmering eyes
We see more mountains in the skies

It takes in many fine reserves
With virgin trees, with bears and deers
It scales the peaks and lofty balds
With balsam, spruce and mountain laurels

We leave the traffic far below
Where tourists seldom want to go
The trickling streams with trout abound
And chattering squirrels are all around

We see great wonders near the balds
We sometimes hear the eagle's squall
Down 'neath the cliffs and evergreens
We often hear wild panthers scream

The rhododendron face the north
You can see them from afar off
Their thrilling beauty draws you near
To fill your heart with nature's cheer

Attractions here are now so great
That folks will come from all the states
To visit those, their scenic rights,
A health resort from business life

The tourists now from southern states
Can enter in at Bryson's gates
At Gatlinburg, both north and west,
Through Newfound Gap can come for rest

So when you come, don't take a chance
Be sure and bring along your "glass"
So you can see away back home
From the top of Clingman's Dome

The balsam, spruce and mountain pine
Sing through the breeze a welcome chime
Come on you tourists, brave and free
Six thousand feet above the sea

Blowing Springs

Over on the Nantahala, about Blowing Spring
We pitched a short vacation, to laugh and talk and sing
Down on the Nantahala, below the mountains large
We spent our short vacation right in the famous gorge

We drove there after supper. We stopped at Blowing Springs
To meet our friends from Bryson, to talk of many things
We talked about the mountains. We talked about the stars
We talked about the waters. We talked about our cars

We listened to the waters. We heard the nightingale
We watched the mighty engine as it crept up the rail
It surely was amusing to watch the engine creep
So slowly up the mountain because it was so steep

We talked about our counties, 'til it was growing late
Then fixing midnight dinner, we all heartily ate
So after we had eaten, we had a lot of fun
We strolled up and down the road, to hear the waters run

They talked about the Smokies. We talked about our town
About our fertile valleys, with assets all around
They claimed they had the entrance into the scenic park
We showed them very plainly that we too had a part

From streams of southern tourists, they sure will have to wait
For them to look through Andrews. We too are on the gate
The tourists we'll entertain when they come streaming through
We'll build for them pretty camps and keep some of them too

They asked about our valleys. They asked about our town
They asked about our factory sites that 'round this place abound
They asked about our quarries of marble gray and blue
That underlies our valley, of which we said "'tis true"

They said they sure was coming to buy some pretty farms
Where they could make a living by growing hay and corn
We welcome them to our town. Now is the time to buy
Come on folks and build up homes before the land gets high

My Seventy-eighth Birthday: A Vacation

We rounded out the Smokies
To see what we could see
And soon we landed safely
Way down in Tennessee

The village where we landed
About a mile around
Was just a little portion
Of Elizabethton

This was our headquarters
For many, many days
Where everything was quiet
And where vacation pays

We went to Watauga dam
The river nearly dry
With many pools and puddles
For fishermen passing by

For up above the valleys
Were many dry land lakes
Was one of nature's questions
How the waters did escape

Me thinks that I can see
Only through my mind's eye
Those kiddies as they romp and play
And I hear them when they cry

While Betty gets away to school
Glenda leaps up on the stone
Poor little T. J. the third
Just has to roll and stroll

We all come back by Knoxville
Though eastern Tennessee
We stopped and ate at Robbinsville
Then into Cherokee

We had a glorious, happy time
As 'round the ponds we roamed
But now it is nice to be
Back at our country home

Note: Betty, Glenda and "Little T. J." were all Tom Thomasson's grandchildren; the children of his son T. J. Thomasson, Jr.

Junior: November 1, 1945

I've got to go to court next week
A juror as of old
I do not mind it very much
If it is not too cold

I've got a good old overcoat
A nice suit as you know
So I will dress up neat and snug
And down the road I'll go

I think I'll make it all just fine
Although a wee bit gray
There's lots of things that I can do
Along life's weary way

The people all have changed about
The courts go on the same
The juror sits up in the box
To tell who is to blame

I dread my job a little less
The nearer that it nears
If I can make it though this court
I may live many years

Junior: November 5, 1945

I got up real soon this morning
And got to court on time
With Judge Ransom on the bench
We dare not be behind

Some nasty things which had occurred
That had to all be tried
Some murder, rape, also rapee
We all had to decide

There are many funny things
And some are very sad
For when the judge says "to the pen"
Some feels mighty bad

Our grand jury has now adjourned
We pushed the business through
The second day we finished up
Then had no more to do

I'm back at home now safe and sound
As happy as can be
If they had known of all my deeds
They might have gotten me

Junior: November 6, 1945

The court up stairs has not adjourned
It's going on there still
We gave them lots and lots to do
By sending lots of bills

If we wish to dodge the courts
We must avoid all crimes
Because there are so many cops
A seeking us – to bind

"If wisdom's ways you'd wisely seek
Five things observe with care
Of whom you speak, to whom you speak
And how and when and where"

"You must observe the golden rule
That is to others do
In all you say or do to them
As you would them do to you"

Now this is all I have to say
To every boy and girl
Be careful what you do or say
And make good in this world

Note: Stanzas three and four are not original to Tom Thomasson. He placed quotation marks around them to denote that. Both phrases appear to be very old rhymes that date at least as far back as the Victorian Era. Some have attributed verse three to C. L. Q. Ingalls.

The Prayer and Faith of Two Children of the
T. J. Hayes Family of Tomotla, NC

I know a Christian mother who was Mrs. Jeff Beal Hayes
She had great hosts of lovers, wherever she was seen
She loved her precious husband. She loved her children too
She always helped her neighbors do all that she could do

She had a model husband who helped folks one and all
Even those who censured him; he helped at every call
She loved her children dearly. She taught them how to pray
Each night before retiring, their little prayers they'd say

She then became afflicted. The doctors said she'd die
The father was then weeping. His children said "Don't cry."
The father kissed their mother. He thought "The last goodbye."
Until they meet together above the starry sky

Two children then was missing, the father got alarmed
Then slipping out to hunt them, he found them in the barn
The children both was praying "Oh, Lord Jesus" now they said
"If you don't help our mama we know she'll soon be dead."

They just kept right on praying, "Lord hear our humble prayers.
Please don't let our mother die. It's more than we can bear."
The father stood and listened, tears streaming down his cheeks
Until the children saw him, he knelt down at their feet

Now Papa we are praying, the Lord we want to tell
Stay with us and help us pray, for Mamma to get well
With his big heart he joined them. He had a lot of faith
In these two praying children, their hearts were full of grace

They all kept right on praying 'til they were satisfied
If they had not been praying, their mamma might have died
But something told them plainly their mother would not die
They hurried back to see her. Their eyes were nearly dry

228

Their mama soon recovered, just as the children pled
To them there was no other, again those two she led
The Lord through these two children, while on their knees they prayed
He told them very clearly their Mamma's life he's saved

Dr. R. L. Madison

There came an educator
From somewhere in the states
To found a teacher's college
And in the mountains wait

He pitched his tent so carefully
He had not long to wait
To see his plans perfected
His ideal was so great

He is a real promoter
The pride of our great state
Who came to Tuckasegee
And taught both soon and late

He is a real instructor
Who teaches as he talks
By precept and example
In all his ways and walks

He is a model teacher
His life has almost spent
To make our future better
Just everywhere he went

He is a splendid mixer
A comrade by the way
To every individual
Has something kind to say

An authority in language
He speaks his English well
If not – it doesn't differ
For none of us can tell

He is a real observer
And does things in a whiz
He is as great in his sphere
As Roosevelt is in his

He is our guest of honor
This day to us is great
About the lake Hiawassee
February is the date

He is our darling Madison
With sparkling eyes so bright
We see him in our visions
While we lie down at night

He lives in Jackson County
About his institute
May he live long and happy
And may his health recruit

Note: The subject of this poem is Robert Lee Madison, a founder of the Cullowhee Academy which ultimately became Western Carolina University (WCU). Professor Madison served as the first and third president of the institution and was associated with the WCU community throughout his life. One copy of this poem has the third from the last verse stricken through. Perhaps the piece was written in anticipation of a speaking engagement by Madison which did not come to fruition.

Tom Thomasson

Our Canadian Mountains

For Miss Bessie: April 10, 1953

Away up in our Canada
the sceneries are so great
They attract many sportsmen
from nearly all our states
Here in Western Carolina
our mountains are our pride
In our spruce and laurel jungles,
wild bear and raccoons hide

Imagine – now we take a hike
up the canyon – zigzag trails
Supposing we are near the crest.
We stop to lunch and take a rest
Then looking up to our surprise,
we see more mountains 'neath the skies
With each other we wonder why,
our mountain peaks are so high

Here mountain laurels hide the cliffs;
rhododendrons with them share
And fragrance from wild roses
fill up the atmosphere
We see great wonders near the balds;
above the peaks the eagle squalls
Down 'neath the cliffs and evergreens,
the vicious panther sometimes screams

The birds up here are singing sweet
and there's humming of the bees
The atmosphere will thrill your heart,
with nature's sweetest breeze
There's babbling brooks and bubbling springs.
There's speckled trout and birds to sing
There's flowers for the honey bees.
There's chattering squirrels up in the trees

Thrilling echoes from the mountains;
thrilling echoes from the hills
Thrilling echoes from the valleys;
thrilling echoes from the rills
The hemlock, spruce and mountain pine
sing through the breeze a welcome chime
"Come on ye people, brave and free,
up five thousand feet above the sea."

Tom Thomasson

Canada, North Carolina

April 10, 1943

This is Canada of which we speak 'tis not up near the North Pole
But high up on Tuckasegee, a place we call our own
This is our Canada, not above the Great Lakes
But up in Jackson County, the pride of our great state

This is Canada here at home; not too hot, nor too cold
A united Canada, where we have gained a goal
Away up here in Canada, high up in the state
Five little schools united, determined to consolidate

Consolidation was the theme, that spread like live wire
The patrons got together and made know their desire
The peppy superintendent, when this great plan was sprung
United all the people an' put all five into one

A building was erected; we had not long to wait
To see the job completed, a credit to the state
A faculty soon selected, began their special work
Each one did well his part, from duty never shirked

The teachers knew their subjects. The students knew their theme
The patrons say "It's working" the best they've ever seen
Here, perhaps, genius is born that may to us unfold
The teachers are optimistic and want to gain the goal

Dear Junior: June 17, 1934

If you still go in swimming, no matter where you roam
Don't get into deep water when you are just alone
Last week there come from Newton a man here to fish and swim
He went down in Santeetlah. That was the last of him

He swam across a channel, was returning back again
His heart then must have failed. He could no longer swim
His party stood and watched him, for none of them could swim
'twas just five feet of water, but that was too deep for him

They dragged the lake and got him. Mr. Gamble was his name
He lacked ten feet of safety, but went down just the same
You must always be careful, no matter how good you swim
When you are in deep water, don't risk a single thing

Echoes around the Great Smokies

Echoes around the Great Smokies, as we look them o'er and o'er
Makes us love the mountains better and praise them more and more
The echoes from the valleys and echoes from the hills
Are the soundings of the hammers and the squeaking of the mills

But some echoes of this region, as we climb the mountains steep
Are those of happy tourists who have nearly reached the peaks
Be sure you see the Great Smokies. The slopes are very steep
But you can reach the summits if you carefully guide your feet

When you have reached the summits, lie down and take a sleep
But you may hear the eagle squall as he flies from peak to peak
Here laurels hide the rugged cliffs. Rhododendrons with them share
And fragrance from wild roses fill all the atmosphere

The birds up here are singing and there's humming of the bees
The atmosphere will thrill you with nature's sweetest breeze
Thrilling echoes from the mountains, thrilling echoes from the hills
Thrilling echoes from the valleys, thrilling echoes from the rills

The echoes from the tourists as they climb the mountains high
Makes each one of them wonder why they mingle with the sky
Up there are fragrant flowers and there's buzzing of the bees
Up here there are babbling brooks and trout darting through the streams

The owl perches on some lofty pine as if talking to his mate
Away down in the canyon, "Hoo, hoo. Up here, for you I wait."
The rhododendrons face the north, their beauties draw you near
You see them from the vale below. They fill your heart with cheer

Now when you reach the summits of many lofty peaks
Lie down and take a slumber and dream about the creeks
When you shall have slept and slumbered you'll say, "Where can I be?"
Awaken by the nightingale, six thousand feet above the sea

Come on you happy tourists where mountain summits rise
To pretty flower gardens among the starry skies
The atmosphere is cooling. The birds are singing here
The honeysuckle's blooming to fill our hearts with cheer

You look down toward the valleys, covered o'er with vulgar clouds
With forked lightening flashing, the vales from us to hide
The tourists find a refuge beneath the shelven rocks
To watch the clouds all vanish below the mountain tops

The Coleman Dam Site

Why not join the motorcade for Knoxville, Tennessee
To advocate Hiwassee Dam in western Cherokee?
We are under TVA, if not in Tennessee
We must help to bring the dam to western Cherokee

We do not want all the dams, like eastern Tennessee
But we must have one mammoth dam in western Cherokee
Such a dam site can't be found, in eastern Tennessee
As nature formed for this plant, way down in Cherokee

Our neighbors now must divide, our neighbor Tennessee
We're her neighbor on the east, her neighbor Cherokee
We must join the motorcade for Knoxville Tennessee
To let Dr. Morgan know we'll yell for Cherokee

Note: This poem has to do with the creation of what is now known as the Hiwassee Dam at Cherokee County, NC. According to Nancy Proctor at the Tennessee Valley Authority (TVA) Library, TVA was founded in 1933 and construction of Hiwassee Dam began in July, 1936. Therefore, this poem was composed within that time period. Three potential dam sites associated with the name "Coleman" were under consideration, along with the nearby Fowler Bend Site. Ultimately, the Fowler location was chosen. Ms. Proctor suggested that "Dr. Morgan" likely refers to Arthur E. Morgan, chairman of the TVA Board of Directors at the time. It is of note that Harcourt A. Morgan, who was a former president of the University of Tennessee, was also a TVA board member during this period of history.

In Memory of Dr. W. C. Mason

November 23, 1953

Our good friend Dr. Mason has gone from us away
To be with God and loved ones, through one eternal day
He was our physician, our neighbor and our friend
We miss his welcome handshake, and his familiar "I wish you well."

A doctor full of mercy, he knew his patients well
He studied well his practice, as everyone can tell
God through his gracious love, taken him from worlds of pain
To a Heaven's bliss above. Our loss is Heaven's gain

He was so kind and devoted. God taken him from us away
To be with Heaven's happy throng, through one eternal day
We are lonely, Oh! so lonely, since he went from us away
But we surely know that we can only look to God for help each day.

Our hearts are sad beyond compare. But we'll submit to God's great will
Heaven's courts rejoice up there. We know He doeth all things well
His active life on Earth is o'er, but his kind deeds live on and on
His soul has flown to Heaven's shore to be with Angels evermore

His lovely voice we do not hear. His smiles we do not see
But in our heart's we have no fear. Those lovely smiles will always be
Our circle now is broken. Our hearts are lonely here
But we'll trust the promise spoken. Oh! May it not be broken there.

Note: Dr. W. Clayton Mason died on October 23, 1953. In addition to being a family friend, he was the father of Leila Mason Thomasson who was married to Tom Thomasson's son Fulton. Dr. Mason fulfilled much of his professional career in the Murphy section of Cherokee County.

Park to Park Way

From park to park we soon can drive
A scenic road up near the skies
The way that nature set apart
To build a road from park to park

The scenery all the way is great
Perhaps the finest in the state
The mountain peaks exceed no doubt
The peaks of any other route

If you've not seen the route outlined
Just keep the Blue Ridge route in mind
If you will look you'll plainly see
Where nature says it ought to be

The Blue Ridge route of which we speak
Is just a chain of lofty peaks
Indeed a scenic rugged crest
That divides the east from the west

The rhododendron here abound
Along the famous Blue Ridge line
The rugged cliffs and waterfalls
Attention to the tourists calls

It takes in many fine reserves
With virgin trees, with bears and deers
It scales the peaks and lofty balds
With balsam, spruce and mountain laurels

It leaves the traffic far below
Where tourists seldom want to go
The trickling streams with trout abound
And chattering squirrels are all around

From Shenandoah, coming south
We cross the Craggie's lofty heights
Still looking up with glimmering eyes
We see Mount Mitchell kiss the skies

With zigzag roads and lofty turns
We drive along through scores of ferns
Through new found gaps we reach the goal
The Smoky park awhile to stroll

We tour the Smokies then loop back
I think we go through Cumberland's gap
To Gatlinburg, the entrance gate,
For Tennessee and western states

The tourists then from all the states
Will come each year to recreate
They'll scale the park and scenic rights
With thanks to Roosevelt and to Ickes

Tom Thomasson

Parkview Service Station

Beyond the Nantahala among the knobs and trees
You'll find a pretty station, with birds and buzzing bees
There you'll see Horace Tabor; six feet, two inches tall
You'll know this smiling fellow, if ever you should call

Be sure and see the cabins the tourists all admire
He keeps them sanitary and has them there for hire
This is a pretty village with Delco lights sublime
To light up every corner and make the cabins shine

Now visit Tabor's Hotel that is arranged so neat
Look out at the Great Smokies before you go to sleep
Now stop at Parkview Station. They have a pretty stock
Be sure and buy your patches at twenty cents a box

Note: The location of Parkview Service Station is not known. It may have been in the western North Carolina/eastern Tennessee region.

Dr. George W Truett

Dr. George W. Truett, of Hiawassee, GA, prayed for and led to Christ the notorious bootlegger of his school boys.

I heard a preacher saying, not many days ago
While he was humbly preaching across the radio
That Truett was out praying, the dealer hiding by
He had two jugs of whiskey Truett's students to supply

The dealer was out lurking, when George went out to pray
He saw the preacher coming and hid himself away
George prayed for him so faithfully he said he thought he'd die
Right there the man repented and broke his jugs of rye

He made a model worker, from then until the end
He loved to tell the story of how and where and when
He thanked Professor Truett and praised him o'er and o'er
He quit the liquor traffic and cut it to the core

He helped to build the college, did all that he could do
To promote all the pupils and other people too
The dealer kept his promise and lived to be quite old
He thought his friends and neighbors should everyone be told

Note: This poem relays events in the life of George Washington Truett, a prominent leader of the Baptist Church who was born in Clay County, NC in the 1860s. Locally he co- founded the Hiwassee Academy at Towns County, GA and served as its first principal. He spent much of his professional life in Texas. He was well known throughout the country. Truett-McConnell College at Cleveland, GA was named in honor of George W. Truett and his cousin/ business associate, F. C. McConnell.

Tapoco

Away down in the canyons, on Little Tennessee
You'll find a pretty village, as nice as it can be
It's away down in canyons, if ever you should go
Surrounded by great wonders. The name is "Tapoco."

They do not have much level land. Great bluffs are all around
That adds much to the beauty, of this nice little town
They have a modern hotel, with everything well fixed
They care for all their boarders and serve them nice and quick

The school here is a model, of boys and girls enrolled
Here, perhaps, a genius was born that may to us unfold
The teachers too are mighty nice. They want to reach their goal
By prizing up the boys and girls, as everybody knows

Now go through the power house; the folks will treat you nice
Look at the generator, that makes so many lights
Climb the steps with Andy Best. You'll reach the top at last
Looking down with dazzling eyes, you'll see the water splash

When you want to go riding, be sure and get a pass
Mr. Perkins will take you, and he won't charge for gas
You'll say when you're boat riding, "That is a great big pond.
It's like the Mississippi, except it's not so long."

If you want to go fishing, go dig a lot of bait
Then tell Mr. Perkins and he will for you wait
Stop at Rhymer's Ferry, if you like big blue cat
You'll get all you can carry, in a great big tow sack

You'll want to stroll the river bed, that now is almost dry
To see the vaults that nature made, with sand and waters high
You'll find lots of pretty stones, as round as they can be
For souvenir paper weights that other folks might see

Now if you should take a hike, you'll find the mountains rough
And if you are not careful, you may fall from a bluff
The folks are very social, as nice as they can be
Always stop at Tapoco, down on the Tennessee

Note: Readers may or may not know the history behind the name Tapoco for the Graham County, NC community about which Tom wrote. It was an acronym for the Tallassee Power Company.

Chapter 9

The Bigger World

COMMENTARY: Chapter Introduction

Newspapers and radio were the primary sources of information in Tom Thomasson's day for people who wanted to know what was going on in the outside world. Tom saw two world wars and numerous other historical events in his lifetime.

This chapter presents significant accounts of history ranging from the American Revolutionary War to the horrors of new atomic weapons which brought World War II to a close. During that era Tom's son, Junior, was deployed with the United States Navy in the Pacific region. With so many other young soldiers gone from the community it was commonplace for loved ones at home to eagerly track the war.

Tom sent a long series of his characteristic "postcard poems" to T. J., Junior while the war was unfolding. On at least one occasion two cards were sent in one day. They were part of a marathon writing session, spanning nearly a month, during the autumn of 1945. Many of these short poems have already been presented in previous chapters of this book.

Mr. Thomasson also kept in close contact with daughter Cora by way of postcard poetry. Cora's letters brought news of troublesome labor strikes from Gastonia, NC where she and her husband were carving out a living. Years later, Tom Thomasson celebrated one of Cora's work supervisors in verse: *Mabelle*. She may have kept in touch with Cora by way of postal letters.

Much of this chapter is filled with writings capturing sadness, uncertainty and grim reflection on the human condition. A moment of pure light-heartedness is included in *Ruth Vacating in Florida*.

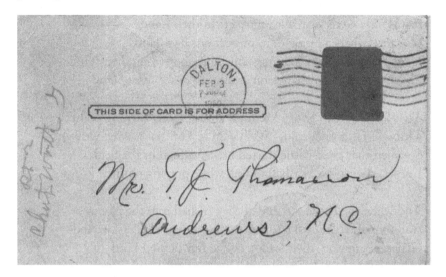

Image 9-1: This "three cent postcard" was addressed to Tom Thomasson in his son John Henry's fancy handwriting. News from the world came in by letter, postcard, newspaper and radio. Even a benign memorandum, like John Henry's assurance that he arrived back at his job safely, was always welcome. Also on this postcard was a message Tom was asked to convey to a neighbor, Mr. Hyde.

Tom Thomasson

The Battle of Kings Mountain

December 11, 1952

It was only yesteryear, with muskets in their hands
Our forefathers all united, to protect our dear lands
It was here with noted courage our brave boys took their stand
To conquer foreign aggression and bring peace to our land

That hill they call Kings Mountain, our bloody turning point
Through faith, they said, "We'll gain it. For that is what we want."
So when that great battle started brave women in the fields
Just left their plow beasts standing while praying on their knees

And when the battle was ended they rushed into the gloom
And tore off their own garments to bind their soldiers' wounds
General Ferguson, their leader, defied our blessed Lord
"All hell," he said "can't take us." He then got his reward

The shot that got the warrior, sent by some unknown hand
Directed by Almighty God was more than he could stand
He tumbled down that mountain side and rolled into a ditch
Just hidden there in trash and mud 'til other graves were fixed

They heaped big rocks upon his grave to make a rustic mound
Engraved his name on one of them that later, could be found
Through faith in God, Supreme Architect, our fathers gained the goal
That coveted United Peace to which we all should hold

Note: Many will recognize the theme of this piece. A historic fight from the Revolutionary War era took place in South Carolina. Thomas Jefferson referred to the skirmish as the "turn of the tide of success."

For Harley Thomasson

I am Harley Thomasson
I'm only just a lad
'twas sad to leave my mother
And my kind and feeble dad

I lived in California
Our greatest western state
The exact place is "Chico"
Where my kindred for me wait

'twas bad to leave my comrades
My girl and all the rest
But thinking of my country
I know that it was best

I like to wear my uniform
It shows just where I stand
Among the many thousands
Who fight for "Uncle Sam"

I like my loyal captain
I'll please him if I can
And do my best for victory
As long as I can stand

There's nothing suits me better
Than fighting for victory's cause
With all united nations
We'll gain the victory, boys

We know that we will conquer
Because we know we're right
It won't take long to lick them
If we all do our mite

Give us ships and planes and tanks
And pray for our success
Give us guns and ammunition
And we will do the rest

We pray for our sailor boys
God bless our marines
Protect – Lord God – our soldier boys
Across the deep blue seas

Note: A number of Thomassons settled in California. Many, including Tom Thomasson's brother Henry Patrick, lived in or around the Butte County region. The exact relationship to Harley Thomasson is not known.

Dear Junior: April 30, 1934

How is C. J. and Cora? We have not heard from them
Since they went from Kings Mountain. What has become of them?
We have looked for a letter from them most every day
Since they left Kings Mountain to go to Gastonia

We don't know what they are doing; guess though they are all right
If they were not they surely would to us something write
We do not know their station or we would to them write
We think about them daily and often too at night

They must be making money and putting in full time
For you see about their writing they're getting far behind
If you see them next weekend, tell them we are all right
And if they have the postage, a post card to us write

Tom Thomasson

Dear Junior: July 27, 1934

I heard about your fishing and heard about your fame
If I could have been with you I would have caught a whale
Though carp fish are much better if they are not so big
Enough of them is plenty to fill a hungry pig

You must have gone to Cape Fear or down upon the tar
Where the water's wide and deep, way down where carp fish are
If so you saw some country that looks much like the west
So I am made to wonder which place you like the best

I think I like the mountains much better every day
Where cyclones seldom come to blow folks all away
If C. J. and Cora moves, you'd better come on too
You have been there long enough, I guess, this time to do

Deflation

F. D. R. closed down our banks
when he saw it was the last chance
We did not know how we'd get by
but now we see that he knows how
He closed them down without a flow
and made for us a better low
"The broke down banks" as they are called
had robbed us all, or nearly all

He called in all the precious gold,
from every vault so we've been told
To stabilize was just his fun
and make for us two out of one
He then pursued with all his aids
a better standard for us made
"Deflation" then said Morgenthau,
"this day becomes our nation's low"

With thirty million now to keep
from desperation and defeat
He split the dollar square in two
to make a half a dollar do
If this don't work we do not know
just what it takes to make things go
With half the money, by the way,
we can near our whole debt pay

With farm notes due and taxes high,
we hardly know how we'll get by
Deflation now has split in two
and with one dollar we now pay two
Our debtor nations now should pay
their war debts here, now by the way
Deflation here has helped them too
so they must pay all they are due

Deflation suits the factory well,
because their products they can sell
Most everywhere it's working fine,
with many mills now on full time
The dollar looks about as big
as when the money all was hid
At any rate it pays the debt
and that's what goes with what we get

Of course the dollar may not buy
just quiet as much as when 'twas high
But dollars cheap or dollars high
with dollars plenty we'll get by
When things are fully stabilized,
then wages everywhere will rise
With times now good in many ways,
we'll give our President the praise

Dear Cora: September 6, 1934

You spoke about the strikers, as though we didn't know
We're reading very careful and know that it is so
The strike is looking shaky, more shaky every day
The worst we've had in history, most everybody says

Some folks won't be satisfied, no matter what mills pay
They always want more money and want a shorter day
When textile mills are going and every hand is trained
To fill the states with loafers is nothing but a shame

If things are not adjusted before so very long
Soup, I guess, will be the diet for many hungry throngs
If things don't soon look better than they do there today
As soon as things admit it, you'd better come away

Tom Thomasson

Mabelle

For Cora: November 7, 1952

Miss Mabelle is our guide each night
She says our work we must not slight
Her hair is red her eyes are bright
She teaches us to do things right

She's never idle, never still
Always patient, never ill
She does her work all in a whiz
As well as Truman can do his

She knows her P's and Q's so well
She just goes through the mill pell-mell
It doesn't take her long to tell
Just how to make the mica sell

We each one do our very best
To make our products stand the test
And please the one that we love best
Because she helps us in distress

She is one of Mica Mill's main stalks
Who teaches as she smiles and talks
She never frowns nor even balks
In all her ways and all her walks

Her conversations are all right
Amusing how she gets about
Not one of use she ever slights
We see her in our dreams each night

When we are parted by and bye
We hope to meet her up on high
Far about the starry sky
There where we no more will die

Emmalou

In Honor of her Graduation: Written June 4, 1945

Methinks I see you, Emmalou, as when you were a child
With pretty golden wavy hair and sparkling bright blue eyes
I remember, too how sweet you sang around your mama's knees
And how your daddy did enjoy the ones you sang for me

I heard of your graduation. It made me mighty glad
I know it pleased your mama and would have pleased your dad
I hope you'll go to college and there to graduate
If you have an engagement he won't have long to wait

I hope you make a teacher, a leader brave and true
Along life's weary journey there is much you can do
If you cannot cross the ocean and the heathen land explore
You can find the heathen nearer. You can help them at your door

Note: Several family members remember "talk of" Emmalou. A handful of letters she wrote to various family members survive. Exactly who Emmalou was has been lost to history. Some think she may have been a family member, likely from Exie's (Tom's wife) side of the clan.

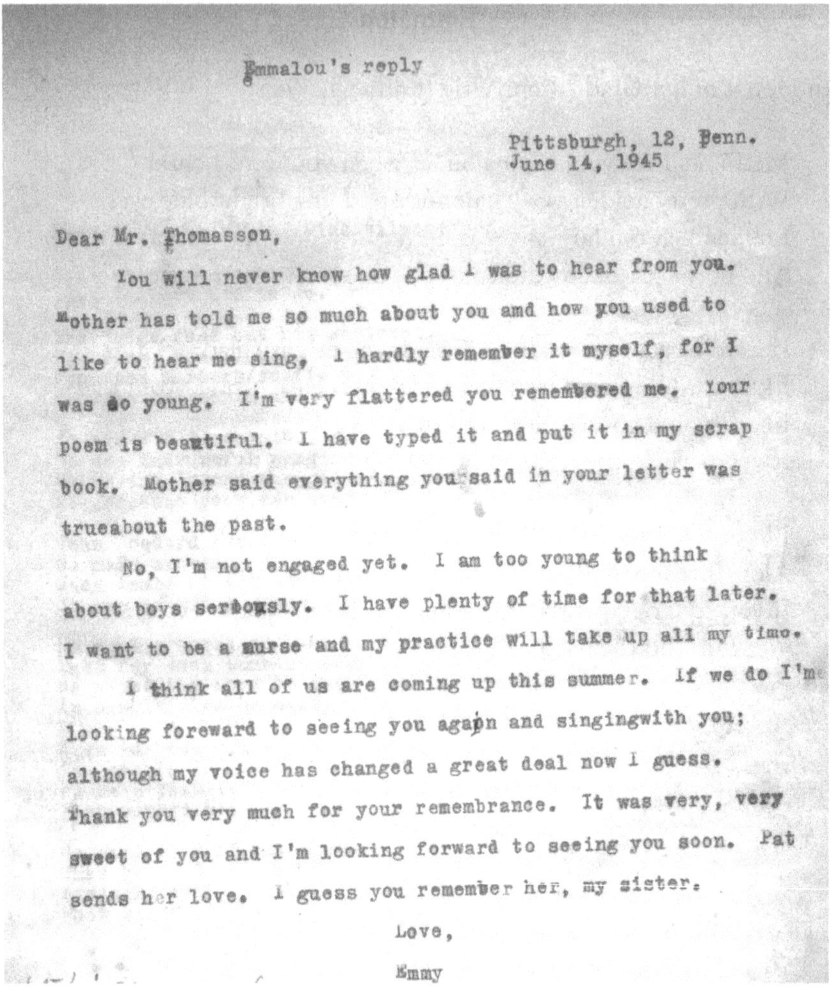

Tom Thomasson

Emmalou's reply

Pittsburgh, 12, Penn.
June 14, 1945

Dear Mr. Thomasson,

You will never know how glad I was to hear from you. Mother has told me so much about you and how you used to like to hear me sing, I hardly remember it myself, for I was so young. I'm very flattered you remembered me. Your poem is beautiful. I have typed it and put it in my scrap book. Mother said everything you said in your letter was true about the past.

No, I'm not engaged yet. I am too young to think about boys seriously. I have plenty of time for that later. I want to be a nurse and my practice will take up all my time.

I think all of us are coming up this summer. If we do I'm looking forward to seeing you again and singing with you; although my voice has changed a great deal now I guess. Thank you very much for your remembrance. It was very, very sweet of you and I'm looking forward to seeing you soon. Pat sends her love. I guess you remember her, my sister.

Love,

Emmy

Image 9-2: In the above letter, Emmalou expresses her thanks to Tom Thomasson for his poem.

Junior: October 13, 1945

The subject now of which I wrote
I guess is getting stale
I guess I'd better change about
And tell some other tale

I doesn't differ though I guess
If all the truth was known
So much about just what I write
Just so you hear from home

I'll study now another text
And let this subject go
The one we wrote so much about
Of which you full well know

It's not the cabin but cyclone
Of which we just now read
That tossed your ship above the waves
That gives us such a dread

We trust that you and yours escaped
The horror of the storm
It still remains for us to learn
The full extent of harm

Junior: October 14, 1945

The great Pacific Ocean
Was named for peaceful tides
But storms are there now raging
Across the ocean wide

We do not know the details
Of all the damage wrought
But we are watching carefully
From all the news that's brought

It shattered Okinawa
Perhaps the worst of all
Because it was the center
Of freedom's greatest call

They may have all decided
With the atomic bomb
That they alone could rule the world
Without the Holy One

We must not defy our blessed Lord
For He is King of Kings
Indeed, our great Commander
He doeth well all things

The Atomic Bomb

Perilous times they have surely come
to every nation 'neath the sun
With nature's products men have won
control of the atomic bomb
We all had better now begin
to ask the Lord for better things
It seems like when we look about
this sinful world will peter out

A mighty weapon man has brought,
perhaps to bring this world to naught
With nature's products men have won
control of the atomic bomb
No doubt some men have got too smart
to build such bombs of nature's parts
Such great destruction no one knows
and no one knows just where he goes

If men had stayed back in their sphere,
such sin we would not had to bear
But for the name of that great prize
some men, perhaps, have gone hog wild
'twill be an awful vulture's feast
when men are slain with every beast
We'll need a place on Earth to hide,
for we can here no more abide

Men should not hurry up the end.
We have no extra time to spend
God in his wisdom knows the best,
when he will take his folks to rest
It matters not if we are right;
to Christ above we'll take our flight
When Gabriel comes the dead will rise
and we will meet them in the skies

Tom Thomasson

To Justify the Atomic Bomb

We've got the tiger by the tail,
with other nations on our trail
So it has brought so much untruth.
We need some help to turn him loose
We realize this bomb is bad;
the sting of which is very sad
The greatest that the world has known,
through Christ we claim it as our own

Two billion is a handsome sum,
to get to use just two bombs
To bring aggression to its knees;
just two bombs fixed the Japanese
We hope the world will plainly see,
we made the bomb for liberty
We did it of our own accord,
to bring all nations great reward

We did not make the bomb for greed
but that the nations we might lead
To higher aims and better things
to which aggressors do not cling
We made the bomb in perfect faith
to save mankind from real disgrace
And protect the weaker ones,
by using the atomic bomb

To show the nations o'er the sea
a peaceful country we will be
We'll keep the secret in our lap,
and the atomic bomb we'll scrap
We'll show the nations one and all
we stood for freedom's happy call
But if aggression comes again
we'll make more bombs and tend to them

Ruth, Vacating in Florida

I'm not a Florida flirty. I'm just down here a while
Vacating with my sister, in this sunny happy clime
This is the land of flowers, with many pretty ponds
Named of, suggested by, Captain Ponce de Leon

I'm not a Florida flipper; I'm not here to relocate
I'm just the same old Ruth I was when I left my native state
While I am here vacating, where streams and oceans mix
I'm thinking of my loved ones, away back in the sticks

I love my dear mother. I love my daddy too
But oh! that pretty boyfriend, God knows I love him too
It has been a great vacation, with beaches quiet and still
But we will soon bid farewell to ancient Jacksonville

Note: The identity of Ruth has likely been lost to history. Some comments about the language in the above writing are of note. The words "vacate" and "vacation" have distantly related language origins but are not very closely linked. In Tom Thomasson's time and place (and among some local people today) these words and their various grammatical forms were often used interchangeably to indicate a trip and/or an extended absence from work. If one were away on a trip, for example, it could be said that she was "vacating" instead of "vacationing." Also, saying that "I will vacate next week" would mean that one was planning a trip or taking time off from their job.

Chapter 10

Of Other Things

COMMENTARY: Chapter Introduction

In the previous chapters of this book there has been a wide assortment of topics and themes stitching together Tom Thomasson's literary vision of the world. From his collections of writing were gleaned tributes to departed friends and neighbors, tales of beautiful gardens and accounts of impish children at play. Tom Thomasson offered narratives on country schools and rhymes concerning meditative nature walks. His song lyrics touched on a variety of themes as well including religion, treasured times at home and even leaving home to see a bit of the world. A key theme or moral could be found shining within the bigger word portrait of these writings more often than not.

In this chapter, the poems are a bit different. The main intention underpinning these creations appears to have been to convey "other things." To clarify, these poems do not fit neatly within the artificial chapter headings of home, family, neighbors and faraway places. All the different sentiments are in place: loss, comedy, longing and pensiveness. The typical rhyme schemes and lyrical patterns are utilized as Tom Thomasson writes of "other things."

Throw Sweet Flowers

Throw sweet flowers up above!
Throw them at the ones you love
Throw sweet flowers all about
They will beat a snap or flout

Throw sweet flowers day by day
Throw sweet flowers by the way
Prize folks up with cheer sublime
Do not try to shove them down

Throw sweet flowers at your friends
Upon whom you can't depend
If you think they won't last long
Throw a bunch and then pass on

Throw sweet flowers every day
As you pass along life's way
They will cheer and comfort give
Throw sweet flowers while you live

Throw sweet flowers in the vales
Throw sweet flowers in our trails
Throw sweet flowers in our homes
They will beat a score of stones

Dear Junior: March 31, 1934

I had my hair cut today
I got a lot of wool
It is just a little gray
And curly as a bull
I put on a brand new shirt
Washed my neck and shaved
I don't think it will hurt
Thought it's been many days

I knew that this was Easter
The best time I could find
So I thought I'd clean up sir
And get it off my mind
I think a man should clean up
At least once every year
If not, he's a dirty pup
And for himself don't care

If I had cleaned up sooner
It wouldn't have been so bad
But looking out for Junior
I thought I better had
That washing sure did help me
It know it very well
If you will try it you will see
And then you sure can tell

A Guy and a Millionaire

On the streets one rainy day
I saw a foolish guy
Calling out, I heard him say
"Who will tote my fry?"

"Ten cents" I think I heard him say
As I was passing by
"To any boy I will pay
To tote across my fry."

That guy had bought a chicken fry
A millionaire standing by
Said "Sir, I'll carry that fry"
Reaching out, he said "I, I"

Across the street with that guy
Plodded he with the fry
Now reaching out said the guy
"Here's pay for toting the fry."

"Thank you very much my son
My name is Vanderbilt
Now when you have more fries to tote
Please call on Vanderbilt"

Note: It is not known if this narrative is based on an actual event.

Tom Thomasson

The Dogwood

The dogwood is an emblem
Of our blessed risen Lord
He was crucified upon it
For sinner's great rewards

The four outspread hearts of white
Represents God's gracious love
A token of the rugged cross
Pointing to His throne above

If you will analyze the petals
You'll see the prints of nails
Four hearts, pointing to the crown
And cross where Christ was slain

The petals show the crown of thorns
With nail prints brown and red
'twas made unfit for cruel deeds
No more by soldiers led

It was the meanest of all trees
As everybody knows
A curse was sent upon it
No more big trees to grow

It is large enough for shuttles
To serve the textile mills
And help out our industry
But causes no more ills

This pretty dogwood flower
That stands against the green
Like the delicate laces
Its like was never seen

268

All of those who know this flower
As each of us well know
Have learned to love and praise it
Just everywhere we go

The real blooming dogwood
With white and pinkish bloom
Was dedicated by our state
But not at all too soon

Now all the dogwood flowers
Seen on our mountainsides
Adds beauty to the scenery
From us they never hide

Its coming was awaited
Its stay is all too short
It's one of nature's beauties
To thrill each of our hearts

A True Story of a Millionaire and His Poor Washer Woman

The millionaire slept and dreamed the third time in succession that the richest person in his county would die next morning at exactly six o'clock. He knew that he was the wealthiest and paid much more than anyone else in the whole county.

The vision was so clear; his nerves immediately broke and he became a wreck. The family physician was immediately called. He tried to comfort him the whole night through.

At exactly six o'clock his telephone rang out. "You're poor old washer woman is dead."

The millionaire then revived, called in his ships and shut down all his factories in reverence to her. He gave his washer woman a millionaire's burial and he spent the remainder of his life in the promotion of God's kingdom here on earth.

The poor old washer woman must have been the richest person in his county.

Dear Junior: June 29, 1934

I'm still budding apple trees, 'bout fifty every day
The time to do anything is when you know 'twill pay
The best time to bud fruit trees is when the sap is high
If you neglect to do it then, the buds are sure to die

There's a time for every job, a time that suits it best
Always try to do that job when you know it pays best
If you do not study well, the things you ought to do
There's many things will be left, that no one else can do

Always put in the best grafts and cultivate them well
The good fruit that they will bear, there's no one here can tell
Do not idle time away for you know it won't pay
Do something good every day. We are not here long to stay

Note: This poem is about more than budding trees but some clarification is offered. An old idea about trees in our area is that the sap would travel upward, within the tree, beginning in early Spring. The sap was said to be at its highest level between June 20 and 22, the day receiving the longest amount of daylight for the year. The ideal time for budding and grafting trees is on that day.

Tom Thomasson

The Electric Fan

The electric fan you sent me was sure enough a treat
We let it blow day and night to keep down excess heat
It was a splendid present, to take it all around
I guess no better than that could anywhere be found

It cools you off so quickly. It's worth its weight in gold
It sings you to sleep so quickly, not many people knows
It pays not off in dollars nor does it pay in cents
But costs a little power, just a very few pence

That fan was a noble trend, indeed a gift worthwhile
If we don't use it too much, 'twill do a little while
It was a fine invention. The inventor knew his beans
For when we touch the button we can rest at our ease

If we don't hear from Sears, I guess 'twill be OK
We'll not talk about it now, but will some other day
He's a mighty nice fellow, with millions in his vault
If he don't get the money, it won't be our fault

Married Girl Blues: 1932

Dedicated to Stella Mae

Mama I will stay at home
From you I never will more roam
I will stay at home sweet home
There's no place like home sweet home

Chorus:
Home sweet home, oh home sweet home. There's no place like home sweet home

You marry if you choose
You will have the married blues
You'll be crying home sweet home
Show me how to get back home

Chorus:
Home sweet home, oh home sweet home. There's no place like home sweet home

I will go to town and buy
I won't stay home and cry
I'll be singing home sweet home
There's no place like home sweet home

Chorus:
Home sweet home, oh home sweet home. There's no place like home sweet home

You will sob and you will mourn
Because your only dress is torn
You'll be crying home, sweet home
Show me how to get back home

Chorus:
Home sweet home, oh home sweet home. There's no place like home sweet home

Tom Thomasson

        I will dress in rayon blue
        And flirt with – you can't guess who
        I'll be singing home, sweet home
        There's no place like home sweet home

Chorus:
Home sweet home, oh home sweet home. There's no place like home sweet home

The Clouds

Andrews, NC: October 10, 1951

I sat alone, gazed at the sky,
where there was naught to change my eye
I watched the clouds as they passed by
to ketch a glimpse of God on high
Me thinks the moisture in the air
forms little clouds up there somehow
Some little clouds just fade away,
others expand with lightening gay

It must have been God's mighty hand
that made those little clouds expand
By drawing water to the land
to help the puny hand of man
His angry wrath the lightening shows;
revealing thunder, 'round us rolls
To show the paths that we must take
to enter through the Pearly Gates

We see His power in the skies
when vulgar clouds above us rise
We fear His wrath down here somehow,
then to His warning we must bow
I wonder why that sinful man
could doubt the power of God's own hand
He made the mountains and the plains.
He forms the clouds that send the rain

We see His beauty in the flowers.
We feel His grace in lonely hours
He hears us when we humbly pray
for He is near us, night and day
This blessed Lord is coming soon.
He's coming all his own to choose
And on the clouds with him we'll ride
to glory where we will abide

Yes, Christ, our Lord, will come again.
On silvery clouds he will descend
To take His jewels over home
where they ever more will roam
Yes on silvery clouds we'll rise
and sail to mansions in the skies
'round stormy clouds no more we'll roam;
we'll be with Christ at home, sweet home

In Voice of the Pumpkin

I am sending you a pumpkin. I mailed it out today
I think that you will get it. I insured it, by the way
I hope you get that pumpkin and that you like it fine
It's like those we ate together. It grew on the same vine

I wrapped it in some papers. Perhaps you'd like to see
To read about the Smokies up where we used to be
Relax and read it carefully and think of Clingman's Dome
Where we climbed up the tower, so far from home sweet home

Come back again next autumn, when pumpkins are all ripe
We'll have another great vacation and take more mountain hikes
This is just a token, to you we would remind
That we would love to have you with us year 'round

Junior #1

Since you have finished college there's still a lot to learn
There's no one here that's perfect. They're found at every turn
If you have passed your subjects, take the right attitude
About the underprivileged; they might have, if they could

Just study human nature. To everyone be kind
Don't think yourself more human than those who're left behind
You can make such people happy with a kind word or smile
Just prize them up a little, 'twill help them every time

There's many underprivileged, if to college they'd be sent
Who would have been quite useful just every where they went
It doesn't pay to censure or knock them if you would
They may have gone to college, if circumstance was good

The idea is to prize them and help them by the way
To do a little better. There's much that you can say
Don't figure folks inhuman because they go astray
Someday they may be useful if encouraged by the way

Autumn

November 12, 1953

The autumn's beauty now we see
In every bush and every tree
Golden leaves of red and brown
Are falling softly to the ground

Amusing – just to watch the leaves
As they fly from mammoth trees
The boys and girls look toward the skies
And chase the leaves as butterflies

Amazing too – that quite a few
Fly up so high above the blue
A Heaven's bliss so very high
They mingle with the starry sky

The brown October has proclaimed
It's time to gather in the grain
Fruits and nuts of golden brown
Are falling gently to the ground

The golden harvest is so great
We have but little time to wait
To gather up with little cost
The precious grain before it's lost

Mother Nature has planned so well
The mountain boomer's instinct tells
They gather nuts and store away
To meet their needs on rainy days

Silly geese through instinct migrate
To warmer climate before too late
But cunning groundhog hibernates
'til coming spring again rotates

The season's eve is drawing nigh
For flowers all do wilt and die
Deep rooted plants will bloom again
About the coming of the spring

As the flowers we too must die
Our evening shades are drawing nigh
But as the leaves we too may fly
To Heaven's bliss in the sky

On the Silvery Clouds

January 1, 1952

On the silvery clouds Christ is coming down
Then Gabriel's trumpet will surely sound
The dead in Christ will every one rise
And sail to mansions in the skies

Chorus:
On the silvery clouds He will come again
To take us from this world of sin
'round stormy clouds no more we'll roam
We'll be with Christ just over home

On the silvery clouds, in the bye and bye
We'll sail to mansions up on high
On the silvery clouds His wings of love
We'll fly to that sweet home above

Chorus:
On the silvery clouds He will come again
To take us from this world of sin
'round stormy clouds no more we'll roam
We'll be with Christ just over home

On silvery clouds we'll fly away home
With loved ones there, we'll ever more roam
And praise His name, all around the throne
While everlasting ages roll

Chorus:
On the silvery clouds He will come again
To take us from this world of sin
'round stormy clouds no more we'll roam
We'll be with Christ just over home

Note: Musical notation for this song is shown in Chapter 7, Image 7-2.

Tom Thomasson

Dear Junior: April 20, 1934

If you have any money, don't take it in your purse
Let someone for you keep it, whom you can fully trust
Your uncle Henry Johnson, soon after he left home
Saved up one hundred dollars and to a robber loaned

There's always little robbers, in nearly every town
And they will take occasion, with you to knock around
The Missus where you're boarding, I'm sure would be alright
To keep your money for you and keep it out of sight

If there is lots of boarders at the place where you stay
Someone might get your clothing and with it get away
Just keep your eyes wide open and never loafer town
So you can keep your money and never be knocked down

Rhymes, Couplets, Quatrains and Quotations

If you will study your own business and let the others alone
You will always find more time to 'tend to your own

Sanding at the foot boys
Gazing at the stars
How can you ever get up boys
If you never try

"I have three sons. One is a professor. One is a…"

A little boy with curly hair
And very pleasant eyes
Did cut down a cherry tree
But would not tell a lie.….
….who was he?

When you are writing anything you can't tell where it will land
Be sure you write nothing you'd care to fall in others' hands

Save the scraps and the chunks will save themselves

If you are building poems don't fail to write the truth
If a lie aimed for a joke, it might mislead some youth

Just do the best you can, for everyone you can, as often as you can

We are all only human
And we all make some mistakes
If you would condemn my work
The right attitude please take

I've tried to do my very best to make this volume beat the rest
I would have if I only could and could have if I only would

Note: Tom Thomasson maintained an extensive library of quotations such as these from the likes of Penn, Luther, Shakespeare, Carlyle, Holmes and many others. The authorship of some remains unconfirmed. Those presented above are believed to be T. J. Thomasson originals.

Forty Years Ago Today: About 1910

November 6, 1950

Just forty years ago today, I stacked a stack of ragweed hay
About the middle of my age, I now must write another page
This page will not be half as long and I will not be half as strong
But to remind us what we have lost, between the two extreme late frosts

So long ago – just to explain, in that first frost I wrote my name
The frost dried up, so did my name and now I may be half insane
But still to us this day is great we've been so active up to date
With little sickness or distress, when life is over our God knows best

It doesn't seem so long ago when I was just a boy, I know
But now I'm old and very grey. The debt of death I must soon pay
But all is well with us we know, when we are called we all must go
To meet the deeds that we have done, where there will be no setting sun

May we be thankful every day and look to Jesus all the way
For everything we do or say the Lord, our God, will always pay
And now may we both great and small, commit our lives to his great call
For bye and bye we all must die, and say to friends, farewell – goodbye

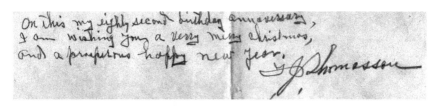

Image 10-1: A holiday wish written by Tom Thomasson in 1952.

References

Barnard, K. (1995). Andrews, North Carolina: Andrews Family Reunion Festival Commemorative History Book. Ann Miller Woodford, Publisher.

Barnard, K. (1996). Andrews, North Carolina: Andrews Family Reunion Festival Commemorative History Book. Ann Miller Woodford, Publisher.

Belcher, S. (2014). 125 Years of Leadership. Western Carolina: The Magazine of Western Carolina University, 18, 3.

Carlin, B. (2007). Helton Brothers/J. D. Harris Discography. The Old Time Herald. Vol. 10, #10.

Ferrell, D. M. (1968). Bear Tales and Panther Tracks, Book Two. Appalachian Publisher, Atlanta, GA.

Ferrell, D. M. (1969). Bear Tales and Panther Tracks, Book Three. Appalachian Publisher, Atlanta, GA.

Freel, M. W. (1956). Our Heritage: The People of Cherokee County, 1540 -1955. Miller Printing Company, Asheville NC.

Holcombe, R. (2014). From a One-Room Schoolhouse to the Millennial Initiative. Western Carolina: The Magazine of Western Carolina University, 18, 3.

Jackson County Genealogical Society. (1992). Jackson County Heritage, North Carolina, vol. I. Walsworth Publishing Company, Waynesville NC.

Jenkins, H. C. & Sossamon, O. L., eds. (1988). The Heritage of Swain County, North Carolina. Hunter Publishing Company, Winston-Salem, NC.

Johnson, B. P. (n.d.). Pullium. Self published.

Lunsford, E. (1996). Ancestors and Descendants of George Washington Lunsford, Carrie Gecona Thompson Lunsford and Ora Augusta Thomasson Lunsford. Self published.

Medford, W. C. (1965). Land O' the Sky: History-Stories-Sketches. Miller Printing Co., Asheville, NC.

Parris, J. (1955). Roaming the Mountains. Citizen-Times Publishing Company, Asheville NC.

Stewart, J. H. (1935). History of the Last Battle of the Civil War, East of the Mississippi River. Unpublished manuscript filed in local public libraries.

Thomasson, C. H. & Malloy, M. B. (1990). Thomasson Traces: Lineage of the Thomasson Family, 1677-1990, vol. I. W. H. Wolfe Associates, Inc, Roswell, GA.

Thomasson, T. J., Sr. & Lunsford, T., eds. (1949). T. J. Thomasson's Book of Poems and Songs, vol. I. Self Published.

Thomasson, T. J., Sr. & Lunsford, T., eds. (1949). Songs, Poems and Declarations Composed and Edited by T. J. Thomasson, Sr., vol. II. Self Published.

Thomasson, T. J., Sr. & Lunsford, T., eds. (1959). Post Card Letters, Poems, Songs, True Stories and Quotations, Edited by T. J. Thomasson, Sr., vol. III. Self Published.

Thomasson, T. J. In Memory of Mother (1909), in Sebren, G. W. (n.d.). Beulah Songs: A Collection of Sacred Songs for All Purposes. G. W. Sebren, Publisher, Asheville NC.

White A., ed. (1987). The Heritage of Cherokee County North Carolina, vol. I. Hunter Publishing Company, Winston-Salem, NC.

White A., ed. (1990). The Heritage of Cherokee County North Carolina, vol. II. W. H. Wolfe Associates, Historical Publications Division, Roswell GA.

White, N. A, ed. (2006). The Heritage of Cherokee County North Carolina, vol. III. Walsworth Publishing Company, Waynesville NC.

Williams, C. H. (2005). Gratitude for Shoes: Growing up Poor in the Smokies. iUniverse Inc., New York.

Wolfe, C. K. (2011). Field Recording Sessions, in Encyclopedia of Appalachia. Retrieved from encyclopediaofappalachia.com.

Printed in the United States
By Bookmasters